How to Write and Give a Speech

Best wishes,

Joan Det

How to Write and Give a Speech

A practical guide for executives,

PR people, managers, fund-raisers, politicians,

educators, and anyone who

has to make every word count

Joan Detz

St. Martin's Press · New York

Design by Mina Greenstein

Library of Congress Cataloging in Publication Data

Detz, Joan.
    How to write and give a speech.

    1. Public speaking.   I. Title.
PN4121.D388   1984   808.5'1   84-11760
ISBN 0-312-39627-9
ISBN 0-312-39628-7 (pbk.)

10   9   8   7   6   5   4

I would like to thank:

PAUL BURNS, who believed in the value of this book
     right from the beginning
TIM YOHN, who wanted to see it in print
MICHAEL DAKOTA, who contributed the cover
     photograph
STUART MOORE, who handled so many details
and BARBARA ANDERSON, who edited this book with
     professionalism and wondrous patience.

Contents

How to Write and Give a Speech

O N E

So You've Been Asked to Give a Speech.... Now What?

Give me a lever long enough, and fulcrum strong enough,
and single-handed I can move the world.

—Archimedes

So, you've just been asked to give a speech.

Do you race to the library to do some research? Do you hunt for some introductory jokes? Do you pull together some statistics? Not if you're smart.

DETERMINE WHAT YOU WANT TO SAY

Begin, instead, by asking yourself, "What do I *really* want to say?" And then be ruthless in your answer. You have to focus your subject. You can't include everything in one speech.

Let me repeat that so it sinks in:

You can't include everything in one speech. In fact, if you try to include *everything,* your audience will probably come away with *nothing.* Decide what you really want to say, and don't throw in any other material.

For example, if you're speaking to a community group about your corporate ethics, don't think you have to give them a complete history of your company, too.

If you're speaking to an alumni group to raise funds for your university, don't throw in a section on the problems of America's high schools.

If you're speaking to the Chamber of Commerce about the need for a new shopping center, don't go off on a tangent about the tax problems of small business.

Get the picture? You're giving a speech, not a dissertation. You can't include every wise thought that's ever crossed your mind.

Remember Voltaire's observation: "The secret of being a bore is to tell everything."

WHAT TO DO IF YOU HAVE NOTHING TO SAY

Suppose—God forbid—that you can't think of anything to talk about? I will give you two anecdotes and two cautions.

> The president of a company called his speechwriter into the room and asked him to write a speech.
> "What about?" the speechwriter asked.
> "Oh," the president said, "about thirty minutes."

Caution: Good speeches do more than fill time. They *say* something.

If you don't know what to say, ask yourself some basic questions about your department, your company, your industry, whatever. Think like a reporter. Better yet, think like a child. Children always come up with great questions—maybe because they aren't afraid to show their ignorance.

- *Who?* Who got us into this mess? Who can get us out? Who is really in charge? Who would benefit from this project? Who should get the credit for our success? Who should work on our team?

- *What?* What does this situation mean? What actually happened? What went wrong? What is our current status? What do we want to happen? What will the future bring? What is our greatest strength? What is our biggest weakness?

- *Where?* Where do we go from here? Where can we get help? Where should we cut our budget? Where should we invest? Where should we look for expertise? Where do we want to be in five years? Where can we expand operations? Where will the next problem come from?

- *When?* When did things start to go wrong? When did things start to improve? When did we first get involved? When will we be ready to handle a new project? When can the company expect to see progress? When will we make money? When will we be able to increase our staff?

- *Why?* Why did this happen? Why did we get involved? Why did we *not* get involved? Why did we get involved so late? Why do we let this mess continue? Why are we holding this meeting? Why should we stick with this course of action? Why should we continue to be patient? Why did they start that program?

- *How?* How can we get out of this situation? How did we ever get into it? How can we explain our position? How can we protect ourselves? How should we proceed? How should we spend the money? How will we develop our resources? How can we keep our good reputation? How can we improve our image? How does this program really work?

- *What if?* What if we could change the tax laws? What if the government deregulates our industry? What if the government doesn't deregulate our industry? What if we build another plant? What if the zoning regulations don't change? What if we expand into other subsidiaries?

These questions should lead you to some interesting ideas.
Need more inspiration? Pick up a trade paper from another
field. Read an academic journal from another discipline. Scan
a magazine that represents a different political opinion. Look
at a foreign publication. Imagine how the readers of any of these
publications would think about your subject.

Or, watch a soap opera you've never seen before. Imagine
how the characters portrayed would look at your subject.

> Albert Einstein, the story goes, was once asked to speak at
> Harvard. After a splendid introduction, he walked to the podium,
> looked at the crowd, paused a long time, and said, "I really have
> nothing to say." Then he sat down.
>
> The audience just sat in stunned silence. Einstein then stood
> up again and promised, "When I have something to say, I'll come
> back."

Caution: Unless your name is Albert Einstein, you probably
won't get away with this approach.

If you decide you have absolutely nothing to speak about
right now, then decline the invitation. Tell the program director
you'd be glad to speak at a later date—when you have more
information to share. Then, keep your word.

Assessing Your Audience

➔

You must look into people, as well as at them.
—Lord Chesterfield

Before you spend one minute researching your topic, before you write one word of your speech, first analyze your audience. This chapter will give you a list of important questions to ask.

FAMILIARITY WITH THE SUBJECT

How much does the audience already know about the subject? Where did they get their information? How much more do they need or want to know?

ATTITUDES

Why are these people coming to hear you speak? Are they *really* interested in the subject, or did someone (perhaps a boss or a professor) require them to attend? Will they be friendly, hostile, or apathetic?

A word of caution about "hostile" audiences: Don't be too

quick to assume an audience will be hostile, and never give a speech with a chip on your shoulder.

Even if the audience doesn't agree with your viewpoint, they might appreciate your open-mindedness, your careful reasoning, and your balanced approach.

A word of advice about apathetic audiences: Some people won't be the least bit interested in your subject. Maybe they're in the audience just because they were obligated to attend, or because it was a chance to get out of the office for a while. Granted, *you* may be interested in your subject, but you'll find plenty of people who aren't.

Surprise them. Startle them. Wake them up. Use anecdotes and examples and humor to keep their attention.

PRECONCEIVED NOTIONS

Will the audience have preconceived notions about you and your occupation? *Remember:* People are *never* completely objective. Emotion often overrules reason.

Try to imagine how the audience *feels* about you.

One effective way to make an impression on the audience is to shock them a bit—to confront and shatter their preconceptions. If you surprise their emotions, you may influence their reasoning.

For example: If you are a social worker, the audience may have a preconceived notion of you as a bleeding-heart liberal, someone with no idea of what social work costs the taxpayer.

Shatter this preconception. Talk about the need to cut administrative costs in social agencies. Talk about the need for stiffer penalties for welfare cheats. Talk about the need for personal and professional accountability in the social work profession.

This approach will surprise—and probably impress—them. They will be more likely to *remember* your message.

Appeal to their emotions to influence their thinking.

SIZE

The size of an audience won't affect your subject matter, but it will probably affect your *approach* to the subject matter.

Small groups (say, up to fifteen or twenty people) and large groups have different listening personalities and different psychological orientations. The wise speaker knows how to appeal to the needs of each group.

People in small groups (a board of directors, for example) often know a lot about each other. They can frequently anticipate each other's reactions to new ideas and problems.

People in small groups tend to pay closer attention to you because it's too risky for them to daydream. They may know you, and they may fear being caught off guard by an unexpected question from the podium: "I haven't been involved in the administration of these loans, but I'm sure Paul Smith could tell us about that. Paul, would you give us the latest details?"

You can take advantage of this small-group attentiveness by emphasizing reason and by offering solid information.

People in large audiences *don't* normally know everyone else. It's easier for them to sit back and feel anonymous. It's also easier for them to daydream.

Speeches to a large audience can—indeed, often *should*—be more dramatic, more humorous, more emotional. Rhetorical devices that might seem contrived in a small group are now useful. The larger the crowd, the greater the need for "a good show."

People in large audiences tend to think, "Okay, recognize me, entertain me, inspire me. Make me feel good about myself when I leave here."

Cater to these needs.

Also, there's one other important reason to ask about the size—big or small—of an audience.

Obviously, if you assume several hundred people will attend, you may feel embarrassed and disappointed when only forty show up. On the other hand, consider this awful experience: a spokesperson for a health organization frequently spoke to small groups of nurses. One time she showed up at a convention and learned she had to speak to a couple of hundred nurses in a large auditorium. She didn't know how to use the microphone. Her slide show wasn't bold enough for the new, large space. And she didn't have enough handouts. Is it any wonder she felt overwhelmed and nervous?

AGE

It's important to find out about the *age range* of an audience and to plan your speech accordingly.

Suppose, for example, you must represent your company at a special town meeting. The meeting starts at 7 P.M., and you expect whole families to attend—including parents with young children in tow.

Now, you may *plan* to talk to the homeowners in the audience about the need for new zoning regulations, but you must also be prepared for the pitter-patter of little feet running up and down the aisles and the shrill cries of babies who want to be fed.

Realize that these distractions are inevitable, and that they will probably occur—alas—just when you get to the most critical part of your speech. If you are mentally prepared for these possibilities (and if you have some friendly one-liners ready), you will be less rattled when the disruptions occur.

MALE/FEMALE RATIO

Some male executives assume that only men go to high-level conferences. When they see women in the audience, they assume these "ladies" are secretaries or, if it's a social event, wives. These men are not big hits among the women executives who happen to be in the audience.

Ask in advance about the likely male/female ratio, and use this information to help you prepare appropriate statistics and examples.

Never, never, make any gratuitous comments about gender or use sexist humor. (Much more about this in chapter 6.)

ECONOMIC STATUS

Suppose you speak as a representative of the local electric utility. An affluent, community-minded group might appreciate hearing about your utility's contributions to cultural groups in the area. But people on fixed incomes won't be impressed to learn you give $10,000 each year to the local philharmonic. They would rather hear about specific ways to cut their electric bills or about your utility's efforts to lobby for "energy vouchers" from the government.

Remember: It's all a matter of perspective. Many of your listeners will be thinking, "What's in this for me?"

EDUCATIONAL BACKGROUND

I once heard an engineer who spoke to all sorts of community groups about his corporation's engineering projects. Unfortunately, he spoke the same way to graduate engineering students as he did to retirees who had no previous experience in the field. You can imagine how well his highly technical speeches went over with the retirees.

Of course, you don't need to change the *point* of your speech. Just talk at a level your audience can understand.

POLITICAL ORIENTATION

Has the group taken an official stand on an important national issue? Did the group actively support a local candidate for office? Does the audience pride itself on being open-minded, or does it take a hard-and-fast view on certain issues?

CULTURAL LIFE

On a Sunday afternoon, would your audience be more likely to visit a museum or take their kids to an amusement park? Would they read *Popular Mechanics, Forbes,* or *Cosmopolitan?*

All of this information will help you understand your audience. When you understand your audience, you'll give a better speech, and you'll have a much easier time with the question-and-answer session.

But, how can you *get* this information about your audience —and get it quickly? Here are nine tips:

1. *Talk with the person who invited you to speak.*   If the host is too busy to help, ask for the name and number of someone who can spend more time with you. Try to talk with this person face-to-face. A telephone conversation is okay, but *don't* rely on a written fact sheet. A fact sheet won't give you insight into the personality of the audience.

2. *Talk with previous speakers.*   See what their experiences were like. What worked? What didn't? What would the speakers do differently if they had a second chance?

3. *Talk with someone who will be in the audience.*   What are these meetings usually like? Who was the audience's favorite speaker? Least favorite speaker? Why?

4. *Ask their public relations department.*   Can they supply an annual report or a newsletter that will give you an idea of the organization's orientation?

5. *Contact the officers of the organization.* (But take their information with the proverbial grain of salt. Officers give "official" information, and rarely provide the candid observations you need.)

6. *Call the reference section of a library.*

7. *If it's an out-of-town speech, ask the local press for some background.*

8. *Use common sense.*

9. *Above all, use a little imagination.*

AN ADDITIONAL WORD TO THE WISE

It's not smart to give the same speech to different audiences. Why?

• You will eventually get tired of presenting the same material, and your boredom will show.

• No two audiences are alike. Your listeners will have different attitudes, special interests, and pet peeves. A direct proportion exists here: the more you try to lump all of your audiences together, the more they will disregard— and even dislike—you.

• You never know if someone in the audience might have heard you give the identical speech somewhere else.

Improbable? Think about this embarrassing situation. One Monday morning at the Waldorf-Astoria, a minister pronounced the benediction before a breakfast meeting of the American Newspaper Publishers Association.

Later in the day, he returned to the Waldorf-Astoria to give the blessing at an Associated Press luncheon. It was—you guessed it—the same prayer, and listeners who attended both meetings were quick to pick up the repeated phrases.

Even worse, the *New York Times* was quick to pick up the story, and ran it under the headline "Invoking the Familiar."

Funny? Sure—as long as it happened to someone else and not to you.

THREE

Where and When Will You Speak?

> At a dinner party one should eat wisely but not too well,
> and talk well but not too wisely.
> —W. Somerset Maugham

After you've determined what your audience will be like, the next step (yes, you should do this before you head to the library and before you put pen to paper) is to consider where and when you will give your speech.

WHERE

Let's start with the basics. Where, *exactly,* will you give the speech?

- In the training center of a large corporation?
- In a university auditorium?
- In a high school classroom?
- In a hotel conference room?
- In a gymnasium?
- In a restaurant?
- On an outdoor platform?

Does it make any difference? Yes.

Plan a Speech That's Appropriate to the Setting

For example:

- If you're speaking on an outdoor platform (as is common at graduations), be sensitive to the weather. Know how to "wrap up" your speech in a hurry if a June thunderstorm cuts you short.

- If you must speak in a large banquet hall, have some one-liners ready for the inevitable moments when waiters interrupt your speech to serve coffee and drown out your words with the clatter of dishes.

- If you'll be in a hotel conference room, bring along some signs reading, "Quiet please—Meeting in progress." Post these signs on the doors to alert people passing through the corridor.

If you've never seen the location, ask the program host for a rough sketch of the room. How big is the area? Where will you stand? Where will the audience sit? Are the chairs movable? "Seeing" all this on paper first will help you feel more comfortable when you actually speak there.

WHEN

Again, the basics. When, *exactly,* will you give the speech?

- At a breakfast meeting?
- At a mid-morning seminar?
- Just before lunch?
- During lunch?
- After lunch, before people return to work?
- As part of a mid-afternoon panel?

- At 4 P.M., as the final speaker in the day's seminar?
- At 9 P.M., as the after-dinner speaker?
- At 11 P.M., as the last in a string of after-dinner speakers?

Plan a Speech That Suits the Time of Day

Use your imagination. Always look at the event from the audience's perspective. What will be on *their* minds?

For example:

- You must be especially brief and succinct at a breakfast meeting. Why? Because your breakfast meeting forced the audience to get up an hour or two early. And because they still face a whole day's work ahead of them. If your speech is not organized and clear and concise—and if they can't get to their offices on time—they will resent you.

- If you speak on a mid-afternoon panel, find out whether you'll speak first or last. Panel presentations run notoriously behind schedule, and the last speaker often feels "squeezed" for time. Be realistic, and be prepared to give a shortened presentation, if necessary.

- If you speak after a banquet (perhaps to celebrate a retirement), know that the audience has been eating and drinking for several hours. They will be in a good mood. They will want to *stay* in a good mood. Don't ruin their evening with an overly long, overly serious speech.

Should You Request a Particular Time Slot?

Yes, if it will improve the effect of your speech.

Suppose, for example, you learn that you're scheduled to speak after a series of award presentations. You suspect, and rightly so, that the audience will be restless after hearing all those thank-you speeches. What should you do?

Be assertive. Let the program host know that you're willing to listen to the award presentations, but that you're not willing to follow them.

If you are showing a movie or slides and will require a darkened room, ask to speak mid-morning or mid-afternoon. Avoid darkened rooms immediately after lunch or dinner. They are conducive to sleep—and the last thing you want is to have your speech interrupted by snores.

A Caution about Out-of-Town Conferences

Know what you're up against. People who travel to a conference in sunny Florida in the middle of January aren't going there just to hear your speech. And people who go to a conference in Las Vegas may not even want to hear your speech at all.

Consider Hubert H. Humphrey's advice for addressing restless audiences:

"You say, 'Buzz-buzz-buzz-buzz-buzz—Franklin Delano Roosevelt! Buzz-buzz-buzz-buzz-buzz—Harry S. Truman! Buzz-buzz-buzz-buzz-buzz—John Fitzgerald Kennedy!' And then you get the hell out of there before they start throwing rolls at each other."

How to Research a Speech

➤

If you cannot get rid of the family skeleton, you might as well make it dance.

—George Bernard Shaw

Now that you've determined the nature of your audience and considered where and when you will speak, the next step is to gather information for your speech. But don't rush off to the library yet. Instead, just sit down and *think*.

USING YOUR HEAD

Your best information source is always *your own head*. Ask yourself, "What do I *already* know about this subject?" Then jot down your thoughts.

Don't worry about organization at this point. Just make some rough notes. Write down important facts, opinions, examples—whatever information you already know. Let your notes sit for a day or two, if possible. Then review them.

Now, begin to look for *specific* information in the form of statistics, quotations, examples, definitions, comparisons and contrasts.

If you don't have enough specifics or enough *variety* of

specifics, do some research and get them. Again, start your research close to home and branch out as needed:

- Go through your files.
- Leaf through magazines related to the subject.
- Consult with friends and business associates.
- Call up a specialist in the field and ask for a comment.
- Introduce yourself to a reference librarian, explain your speech assignment, and ask for resources.

MAKING GOOD USE OF THE LIBRARY

Reference librarians are invaluable to any speechwriter. Absolutely invaluable. They know their way around a library and can save you countless hours of time and frustration.

Many reference librarians even handle inquiries over the telephone. If this service is available at your local library, keep the telephone number handy.

If you expect to give many speeches during your career, become friendly with a reference librarian. Take a reference librarian to lunch. It's a worthwhile investment in your career.

Another worthwhile investment? Become familiar with some basic reference books. I've included a list of basic reference books at the end of this chapter. They will help you write better speeches—and they will help you do it faster.

These reference books are widely available in public libraries, but if you write a lot of speeches you will want to buy some of them for your personal library.

WHAT TO LEAVE OUT

As the speaker, you're in control: *you* get to choose the precise topic. You also get to decide what information stays and what information goes. What *not* to say is just as important as what *to* say.

Leave out:

- irrelevant details
- boring details
- any information you can't verify
- anything you wouldn't want to see quoted in print the next day
- anything you wouldn't want to be reminded of next year

APPROACHING THE TOPIC FROM THE AUDIENCE'S PERSPECTIVE

Your audience can understand your subject only by relating it to their own ideas and problems and experiences. So, approach the subject from *their* perspective, not *your* perspective.

For example, don't just complain about your industry's problems. Even if you have some legitimate complaints, your audience will probably not care. They have enough problems of their own.

Instead, relate *your* concerns to *their* concerns. Find the emotional "hook" that will help the audience understand your message.

Talk about audience *benefits.* Show how the audience would benefit if your industry could solve its problems. Would the audience save money? Save time? Be healthier? Be happier?

Approach the topic from their perspective, and you'll be more effective. It's a fact: audiences tend to trust—and to like —speakers who show a real understanding of them.

HOW TO USE STATISTICS FOR IMPACT

Some people think statistics are boring. These people have not heard the right statistics.

Statistics can be downright interesting, *if* you:

1. *Make the statistics seem real to your audience.* Try, "While we're sitting here for an hour and debating the value of sex education in the schools, 'x number' of teen-age girls will give birth to illegitimate children."

   Or, "While you're watching your favorite TV show tonight, forty-five people will call the national cocaine hotline to ask for help. Could one of them be *your* child?"

2. *Explain what your statistics mean.* Here is how John Anderson, president of Farmland Industries, explained agricultural productivity to the Society of American Business and Economic Writers:

   In 1950, the American farmer fed fifteen people. Now, he feeds sixty-five. The number keeps growing. What does this mean to the 97 percent of Americans who are not on farms? It means they don't have to work so long to get the food they need. The average wage earner in 1950 worked ninety-four minutes to buy the food that can be purchased today with just sixty minutes worth of work. . . .

3. *Put statistics in simple terms.* Don't just say that your senator will mail "x" million items to his constituents this year. Instead, explain that this amounts to about three deliveries to every mailbox in his district. Everyone who has a mailbox can relate to that statistic.

4. *Round off the numbers.* Say "almost one million customers," not "997,755 customers." Make it easy for the audience to *hear* and *remember* your statistics.

5. *Use numbers sparingly.* Audiences cannot absorb more than a couple of numbers at a time. If you use too many statistics, you will lose your listeners.

6. *Be graphic.* Try to paint a picture with numbers. That's what James R. Fullam, vice president of the Sperry Corporation, did with this statistic about building the Epcot Center:

> The construction work required moving fifty-four million cubic feet of earth to fill what was once a swamp. That meant moving enough earth to fill the New Orleans Superdome.

Most listeners wouldn't understand "fifty-four million cubic feet of earth," but they *could* visualize the amount of earth it would take to fill the New Orleans Superdome. So, be graphic. Paint a picture for them.

7. *Do not apologize for using statistics.* Inexperienced speakers often say, "I hate to bore you with statistics, *but. . . .*" After this apology, they proceed to bore their audiences with poorly chosen and poorly used statistics.

Avoid this pitfall. If you follow the guidelines in this chapter, your statistics will *not* be boring. They will, in fact, add a lot of interest to your speech.

HOW TO USE QUOTATIONS

Audiences love quotations, *if* you:

1. *Use some variety.* If you're speaking about productivity, for example, don't just quote the U.S. Department of Labor. Use a variety of sources. Try:

   • Abraham Lincoln ("My father taught me to work; he did not teach me to love it.")

- Robert Frost ("The world is full of willing people; some willing to work, the rest willing to let them.")
- The Bible ("The harvest truly is plenteous, but the labourers are few.")
- The president of a local union
- The manager of a large personnel department
- An industrial psychologist
- An anonymous commentator ("People come up to me and say, 'Yours is the best-run factory in the United States.' And that makes me feel great. But I know our productivity will start to decline if we ever become too proud or too careless.")

2. *Avoid lengthy or complicated quotations.*   Keep quotations short. Cut or paraphrase any "slow parts."

3. *Blend the quotation into the text.*   Never say "quote . . . unquote." Instead, pause a moment and let your voice emphasize the quotation. Or, better yet, blend the quotation right into the preceding sentence. Here is how Donald R. Stephenson, director of corporation communications for Dow Chemical Canada, Incorporated, handled the situation:

> Samuel Johnson said that when a man knows he is to be hanged in a fortnight, it concentrates his mind wonderfully. That's the way it is with management. When a crisis breaks, their minds are focused wonderfully—and that's your best chance to get their attention and win their respect.

4. *Appear comfortable with the quotation.*   Never quote anybody unless you're sure you can pronounce the name right. I once heard a speaker quote "the well-known German writer, Goethe." Unfortunately, he pronounced the name as "Goath"—and the quotation just fell flat.

5. *Use quotations judiciously.*   A speech should reflect *your* thoughts and expertise, so don't quote dozens of other

people. In a fifteen-minute speech, you can probably use two or three quotations. Remember: The impact of your quotations will decline sharply as their number grows.

HOW TO USE DEFINITIONS

What do you mean when you speak about "liquidity problems"? About "decreasing profit margins"? About "a captive finance company"?

1. *Define your terms in everyday words.* Avoid "dictionary" definitions. "According to Webster, . . ." is a phrase that sounds feeble and amateurish.

2. *Try a definition with a light touch.* You might want to ask a six-year-old for a definition of "management compensation" or "gun control" or "inflation." You'll get some amusing definitions that could add interest to your speech.

HOW TO USE COMPARISONS AND CONTRASTS

Here is a contrast from Leonard N. Mackenzie, chairman of General Automation, Incorporated, in a speech on the need for computer literacy:

> In researching this talk, I was struck by the fact that the United States, the free world's leader, and the world's yardstick economy by far, boasts a nearly universal traditional literacy rate. . . .
>
> In economically depressed Zimbabwe, by contrast, just 30 percent of the population is traditionally literate. In the African republic of Malawi, only 25 percent of the population can read

and write—and the per capita annual income is a numbing $220. . . .

And, what I'm saying is nothing less than that much of today's adult workforce finds itself facing a "Zimbabwean" economic future *unless* we mount a hard-hitting, comprehensive computer literacy crusade for today's workers.

Choose your comparisons and contrasts carefully. If you try to compare apples and oranges, your comparison will be meaningless.

HOW TO USE EXAMPLES

Examples can be interesting. Unfortunately, they can also be misleading. President Reagan once cited the example of a "welfare queen" who used false names to collect multiple benefits. However, he failed to show that this example was *representative*. He failed to prove that the "welfare queen" was typical of people who get government aid. In short, he failed to use an example properly.

Always remember: An example is *not* proof. If you use an example, make sure it gives the audience a fair picture of the situation. Otherwise, you will lose your credibility.

SOME FINAL THOUGHTS ABOUT RESEARCH

Sophisticated listeners will question the source of your information. Make sure the source is *reputable* and *appropriate* for your particular audience.

Also, be sure to use a *mixture* of material in your speech—maybe one or two quotations, an example, a couple of bold statistics, and a comparison. This variety will make your speech more interesting and more credible.

Be aware: Some people just don't assimilate certain types of information. "Numbers people" may consider anecdotes "frivolous" or "invalid." "People people" may mistrust statistics, preferring to receive their information in anecdotal form. Use a combination of techniques to get your message across.

SOME USEFUL REFERENCE BOOKS

Quotations

Peter, Dr. Lawrence J. *Peter's Quotations: Ideas For Our Time.* New York: Bantam, 1980. $3.50   A great collection of quotations—from Martin Luther to Henry Ford to Woody Allen. Most entries are brief and witty—ideal for a speech.

Safir, Leonard, and William Safire. *Good Advice.* New York: Times Books, 1982. $16.95   Two thousand bits of advice from ancient and modern sources on such topics as achievement, conciseness, prosperity, and talent. An invaluable resource for speechwriters.

Charlton, James, ed. *The Executive's Quotation Book.* New York: St. Martin's Press, 1983. $9.95   More than 400 quotations about the business world. Where else, for example, could you find Casey Stengel's observation on management: "The secret of successful managing is to keep the five guys who hate you away from the five guys who haven't made up their minds."

Lewis, Alec. *The Quotable Quotations Book.* New York: Cornerstone, 1981. $12.95   This is not the place to find out what Wordsworth said about daffodils. But if you want lively comments on contemporary subjects—from advertising to computers to pollution—this book will give you 2,800 quotable quotations.

Fergusson, Rosaline, ed. *The Penguin Dictionary of Proverbs.* Middlesex, England: Penguin, 1983. $5.95

Auden, W. H., and Louis Kronenberger. *Viking Book of Aphorisms.* Middlesex, England: Penguin, 1981. $6.95

Bartlett, John. *Familiar Quotations.* Edited by Emily M. Beck. Boston: Little, Brown, 1980. $29.95   Passages, phrases, and proverbs from ancient and modern literature. Arranged chronologically by author. A standard literary reference work, but many of the selections are too long to work well in a speech.

Clapp, James. *The City: A Dictionary of Quotable Thought on Cities and Urban Life.* Piscataway, New Jersey: The Center for Urban Policy Research, 1984. $30   More than 3,000 quotations about cities from more than 1,000 writers. Invaluable for speakers who want a "local color" reference for out-of-town speeches. Contains an authors index, a subject index, and a cities index (covering more than 300 cities from Accra to Zurich).

Woods, Ralph L., ed. *A Third Treasury of the Familiar.* New York: Macmillan, 1980. $29.95   This book contains thousands of literary and historical entries. One of the gems is William Faulkner's resignation as postmaster: "As long as I live under the capitalistic system, I expect to have my life influenced by the demands of moneyed people. But I will be damned if I propose to be at the beck and call of every itinerant scoundrel who has two cents to invest in a postage stamp. This, sir, is my resignation."

Statistics

Lane, Hana U. *The World Almanac and Book of Facts.* New York: Newspaper Enterprise Association, 1984. $4.95 The best American book of facts. Almost 1,000 pages. Excellent index, with both general subject headings and specific names. This book has been on the desks of newspaper editors for generations; it's also a "must" for home and office libraries.

Asimov, Isaac. *Isaac Asimov's Book of Facts.* New York: Grosset & Dunlop, 1979. $12.95   Three thousand unusual bits of information in almost 100 different categories, from energy to military secrets to fashions.

U.S. Bureau of the Census. *Statistical Abstract of the United States.* U.S. Government Printing Office, annual. $11 Gives statistical tables on demography, economics, finance, and population. To order, call the GPO at (202)783-3238 (credit cards accepted). Or, write to the Superintendent of Documents, U.S. Government Printing Office, Washington, DC 20402.

Wasserman, Paul, and Jacqueline O'Brien. *Statistical Sources.* Detroit: Gale Research Company, 1984. $160 A subject guide to industrial, social, educational, and financial data on thousands of topics. It will tell you where to find information on palm oil production in the Congo—and other more basic subjects.

General Reference

Todd, Alden. *Finding Facts Fast.* Berkeley, California: Ten Speed Press, 1979. $3.95 A first-rate book for anyone who wants to learn the basics of research. Easy to read and use.

Bell, Marion V., and Eleanor A. Swidan. *Reference Books: A Brief Guide.* Baltimore: Enoch Pratt Free Library, 1978. $3 The most useful list of reference books available. Order it by mail from the Enoch Pratt Free Library, 400 Cathedral Street, Baltimore, MD 21201. Enclose a check.

Akey, Denise S. *Encyclopedia of Associations.* Detroit: Gale Research Company, 1984. $160 A best-selling reference book—and with good reason. Locate it in your local library and *use* it. This encyclopedia describes more than 16,000 trade and professional associations. It gives the names and telephone numbers of people in these associations who can give you current statistics and opinions on thousands of topics.

Congressional Directory. U.S. Government Printing Office, annual. $12 Definitive guide to Congress and its committees, federal courts and judges, agencies and officers of the Executive branch. Gives the names, addresses, and telephone numbers of people to contact at these offices. To order a copy, call the Government Printing Office Bookstore at (202)783-3238 (credit cards accepted). Or, write to the Superintendent of Documents, U.S. Government Printing Office, Washington, DC 20402.

Evans, Ivor H. *Brewer's Dictionary of Phrase and Fable.* New York: Harper & Row, 1981. $24.95 A gold mine of wonderful trivia about popular phrases, fables, romances, archeology, history, religion, the arts and sciences.

Kane, Joseph Nathan. *Facts About the Presidents.* New York: H. W. Wilson Company, 1981. $28 A quick reference to events and dates in U.S. history, organized by presidential administrations.

Hatch, Jane, ed. *The American Book of Days.* New York: H. W. Wilson Company, 1978. $60 What happened and when.

Creativity

Osborn, Alex. *Your Creative Power: How to Use Imagination.* 1948. Reprint. New York: Scribners, 1972. $20 A classic. A first-rate, detailed, and informative book—invaluable for people who must come up with ideas. Written by an advertising man: he was the *O* in B.B.D.&O., the famous advertising firm of Batten, Barton, Durstine and Osborn.

Young, James Webb. *A Technique for Producing Ideas.* Chicago: Crain Communications, 1975. $4.95 A short classic by an advertising pioneer. It's been around for more than 40 years—and with good reason. Read it for inspiration.

Writing the Speech

Begin at the beginning and go on till you come to the end;
then stop.
—The King, in *Alice in Wonderland*

All right. Enough thinking, enough planning, enough researching. Now's the time to sit down and write.

What do you have to do to write a good speech? Two things:

1. Make it simple.
2. Make it short.

What do you have to do to write a *great* speech?

1. Make it simpler.
2. Make it shorter.

In this chapter, I'll tell you how to make your speech simple and easy to understand. In the next chapter, I'll show you specific techniques to make it short—and memorable.

These two chapters are the guts of the book. Read them carefully. Re-read them with a pencil in your hand. Mark the hell out of them. Because they tell you everything this professional speechwriter knows about writing speeches.

THE NEVER-FAIL FORMULA

Here's the formula for a successful speech. It works every time.

- Tell them what you're going to tell them.
- Tell them.
- Tell them what you've told them.

TELL THEM WHAT YOU'RE GOING TO TELL THEM: THE INTRODUCTION

I won't mince words. The introduction is the toughest part. If you don't hook your listeners within the first thirty seconds, your cause is probably lost.

Start with a "grabber"—an anecdote, a startling statistic, a quotation, a personal observation, a literary, historical, or biblical allusion. Use whatever it takes to get the audience's attention. Give them a good taste of what's to come.

It can be risky to begin a speech with a joke. If it falls flat, you're off to a terrible start, so don't use a joke unless you are *absolutely* sure you can deliver it well. Even then, use a joke only if it's short and if it relates to the topic of the speech.

Never, *never,* open by saying something like, "I heard a really funny story today. It doesn't have anything to do with my speech, but at least it'll give you a good laugh."

Instead, try one of these opening techniques:

Make Up a Good Anecdote

Lots of reference books list anecdotes for speakers to use. Be careful of these sources. The anecdotes often sound contrived. Indeed, they *are* contrived.

You're better off making up your own anecdotes—for several reasons:

1. If you speak from personal experience, you can be pretty sure the audience hasn't heard your anecdote before.
2. You'll remember the story better and be able to deliver it more effectively.
3. You'll come across as more sincere.

When the "I Love New York" advertising campaign was getting under way in the late 1970's, Jane Maas, a spokesperson for the campaign, used this personal anecdote to open a speech:

> I was in Albany yesterday morning, having breakfast in the hotel coffee shop, and a cute little waitress spotted my button and came up to me and said, "I'm from Georgia, but I *love* New York." And I thought to myself, "Goodness, we are *living* the commercial."

Caution: If you decide to use anecdotes from a source book, be sure to change them slightly before you put them in a speech. Personalize them. Make the stories sound as if they actually happened to *you.*

Try Candor

When Reuven Frank, senior executive producer for NBC News, spoke to a news directors' association, he admitted it was a new experience.

> Since I am not myself a goer to conventions, this may be the first keynote address I have ever heard. I'm flying blind. You will forgive me if I do it wrong. I'm no longer good at pep talks. I have no idea what the future holds. In fact, I know more about what television news used to be than what it is now.

Challenge a Common Misconception

When author Caroline Bird spoke to the Institute for Managerial and Professional Women, she began her speech by challenging the popular image of a family.

> People are always asking me, What is the women's movement doing to the family? And I always answer: What family do you mean? If you mean the family that is on the logo of the Family Service Association of America, that family is gone forever. It's the one that is depicted by a breadwinning father and a homemaking mother with two little children hand in hand. Only 7 percent of American families now answer to that description.

Admit Disappointment

Did you lose an account? A big case? A contract?

Disappointed? Damned right you are. Admit it. Then move on—*quickly.*

When Ted Kennedy lost the Democratic nomination for President in 1980, he opened his concession speech this way:

> Well, things worked out a little different from the way I thought, but let me tell you, I still love New York.

Show a Real Understanding of Your Audience

John Ong, chairman of B. F. Goodrich, showed a genuine understanding of his audience when he spoke to the Graduate School of Management at Purdue University:

> I understand you have an intensive orientation schedule this week, and I know you have a rigorous course of study facing you in the months ahead.

Of course, one would expect nothing less from one of the top management schools in the country.

That's not something I'm saying just because I happen to be here this morning and feel the need to be polite. I say it because at Goodrich we have a genuinely high regard for the programs at Purdue, both in management and in the engineering and science disciplines. Goodrich has recruited here for many years, and a large number of Purdue graduates have joined the company.

Tease the Audience (But Just a Little)

When Ronald Henderson, president of the Medical Association of the State of Alabama, spoke to the Alabama Hospital Association's 61st Annual Convention, he opened his speech with a bit of teasing:

> I was told that you would provide transportation, hotel room, someone to meet me at the airport to bring me to the Convention Center. . . . But no one said anything about seeing me out. I sincerely hope that this was due to the fact that I am leaving quite early in the morning for Chicago, and not because of your concern about what I might have to say today.
>
> With that in mind, I would like to say, at the beginning, that some of my best friends are hospital administrators—and I hope that will still be the case when I leave Mobile.

Promise to Be Brief

If you promise to be brief, you immediately have the audience on your side. Here's how Howard Love, president and CEO (chief executive officer) of the National Steel Corporation, opened a speech in Detroit:

> After the long and grueling primary races and the recent presidential election, I'm sure the nation's key speakers are ex-

hausted. I'm equally sure that you, the listeners, are exhausted, as well.

So, with sympathy for your overtaxed ears, I remind myself that the secret to survival for speakers at The Economic Club of Detroit is similar to the survival of the pedestrian in downtown Detroit traffic: there are the quick . . . and the dead. I plan to be quick!

One important point: If you promise to be brief, keep your word.

Play with the Title of Your Speech

BankAmerica's president, Samuel Armacost, used this opening when he spoke to the Fowler-McCracken Regional Leadership Conference in Los Angeles:

> The title I've given this keynote address is "The Road to Renewal." Now, I suppose that this close to Hollywood, when you hear something called "The Road to . . ." you're in the habit of expecting Bing, Bob, and Dorothy. Well, no such luck. Actually, this production, the economic renewal of America, stars you . . . me . . . all of us.

Openings for Special Circumstances

If you are a substitute speaker . . .

So, you're a last-minute invitee? Get it out in the open, and move on.

John J. Holton, vice president, marketing, of the Burroughs Corporation, used a light touch in this situation:

> On behalf of Burroughs Corporation, thank you for your invitation. I admit that I lack the fame and the TV stardom of Carl Janzen, the original invitee. Still, I'm reminded of the observation

once made by Woody Allen: "Showing up is 80 percent of life." If he's right, then this talk is already four-fifths of a success.

But, I want to do more tonight than just show up. I want to contribute to the mutual understanding of business and academe. I want to help bring down that wall that some people say stands between us.

If you've spoken to the group before . . .
From President Ronald Reagan at the United Nations:

Thank you for granting me the honor of speaking today, on this first day of general debate in the 38th session of the General Assembly. Once again I come before this body preoccupied with peace. Last year I stood in this chamber to address the Special Session on Disarmament. I have come today to renew my nation's commitment to peace. I have come to discuss how we can keep faith with the dreams that created this organization.

If the listeners are experts and you are a generalist . . .
Stephen Dorne, president of the World Health Alliance, addressed the World Health Convention with:

Since I am not a doctor or a scientist, and many of you are, my task here today is somewhat delicate. Furthermore, I am adamantly opposed to "instant experts" who make all sorts of pronouncements on all sorts of subjects . . . they know little about. So, I will take refuge in Alvin Toffler's analogy of the eye: the expert supplies the focus, while the layman provides the peripheral vision.

If the audience has already heard many speeches about your subject . . .
Joseph Reid, president and CEO of the Superior Oil Company, took a direct approach when he spoke to the Houston Association of Petroleum Landmen:

You and I have heard it all already. The energy crisis . . . the need for domestic energy supplies . . . OPEC . . . government bureaucracy . . . and on . . . and on. We've heard it all. We know it too well. We've told it to each other in places like this . . . and we've listened to others tell it.

So, what's the matter? Why is it that Americans still don't believe there's a real energy crisis? Why is it that the oil industry is still our favorite national villain? If we're so right, how come nobody listens?

If you have taken a new job since accepting the speaking engagement . . .

Here is how Marc LaLonde addressed his new position as Minister of Finance of Canada:

I am sure you won't be too disappointed to have invited the Minister of Energy and received the Minister of Finance instead. I can assure you that since changing portfolios I have not encountered any shortage of things to talk about.

This is, in fact, my first official speech as Minister of Finance.

If you are a white speaker addressing a predominantly black audience (or vice versa) . . .

When William Agee, CEO of the Bendix Corporation, spoke to the Black M.B.A. Association in Detroit, he established a common bond right at the beginning:

The purpose of the National Black M.B.A. Association is to widen the door to middle and top management and the board room for black executives. I applaud that purpose, and I am proud that, as a charter member of your organization, Bendix has supported your efforts from the beginning.

If you are speaking out of town . . .

Avoid this all-too-common opening: "It's great being here in Cincinnati/Philadelphia/Walla Walla."

The first thing your audience wants to know is "Why?" "Why on earth," they're saying to themselves, "are you so thrilled to be here in Cincinnati/Philadelphia/Walla Walla?"

Were you born here? Did you go to college here? Did you start your first job here? If so, then *tell* the audience. They'll appreciate the personal connection.

Ruth Bryant, vice president of the Federal Reserve Bank of St. Louis, used this personal opening when she returned to Memphis, her hometown:

> Thank you for the opportunity to return home to Memphis on behalf of the Girls' Clubs. . . .
>
> I was born in Memphis and grew up here. For the last several years, although I have lived in St. Louis, I have come here frequently to our branch of the Federal Reserve Bank and to visit friends and relatives, and I still consider this my home.

An audience will also appreciate hearing about a *business* connection to their city. If you have one, tell them. If you don't have one, you'd better come up with one.

Philip Caldwell, chairman of the Ford Motor Company, used this:

> I am especially pleased to be here today because, among other things, Ford Motor Company has an important stake in Indiana. We make things here. We buy things here. We sell things here. And from time to time—at Indianapolis—we race things here.

Some Cautions about Beginning a Speech

It's not necessary—or even desirable—to begin with: "Good evening, ladies and gentlemen." Greetings like this are really just fillers. Skip them. Jump right in with the first line of your speech.

The same goes with most introductory *thank you*'s. They can sound pretty feeble, and feeble is not the way to begin a speech. Whatever you do, avoid trite openings. Almost every run-of-the-mill (read: boring) speech begins with something like, "It's such a wonderful pleasure to be here today." Who is this speaker trying to kid? Since when is speechmaking such a pleasure?

Everyone knows that giving a speech is hard work. Most people would rather do *anything* than stand up and give a speech.

Don't flash a phony smile and open with a glib line. Audiences are quick to spot insincerity. And they're slow to forgive you for it.

If you're really enthusiastic about giving your speech, it will show in your content and delivery. You won't have to fake it with flowery openings.

TELL THEM: THE BODY

Inexperienced speechwriters want to say everything, and that's where they make their first mistake. Focus your material, and limit the number of points you make. If you concentrate on one central idea, your audience will stand a better chance of understanding you.

Wait a minute. Are you saying to yourself, "But my topic is so important, I've *got* to get everything across"?

Don't get carried away with your own importance.

If you try to say *everything,* your audience will come away with *nothing.* It's as simple as that.

No matter what your speech is about, you must limit, focus, and organize your material. There are lots of ways to do this. Use whatever method works best for you.

Chronological Order

Try dividing your material into time units—from past to present to future—or whatever pattern seems to fit. This method can be effective because it *connects* everything. For example: If a new tax law adversely affects your company, review or predict its effects at ten-year intervals. Start with the present, perhaps, and show how the law hurts your business today. Then go back ten years—before the law went into effect—and show how your company was better off. Take the offensive law ten years into the future and predict how it will hurt your company then. Will you have to lay off employees? Will you have to reduce your contributions to local cultural groups? Will you have to stop production on a new plant?

Show how historical changes affect the quality of people's lives. If possible, show how these changes affect the quality of your *audience's* lives.

Cause and Effect

Did you start an employee program that has produced positive benefits throughout the company? Then say, "I'd like to tell you about our new Employee Suggestion Plan. It's a success, and it has improved productivity in all seven departments of our company."

Did something go wrong with your marketing plan and cause problems elsewhere? Use that cause-and-effect relationship to organize your speech.

Was your transportation section able to reduce its gasoline costs this year? Tell what caused that improvement: downsizing, better maintenance, more efficient routes, etc.

Numerical Order

You can go from the highest to the lowest number, or from the lowest to the highest.

Suppose you want to show how your volume of oil production has increased. Look at the numbers as part of an escalating trend. Relate them to specific events so the audience can see *why* your oil production went up.

Suppose you want to show how theft has been reduced in your distribution department. Explain to your audience *why* those numbers went down.

Always relate numbers to *human* events. That's the only way they will make sense to your audience—which will, presumably, be composed largely of humans.

Problem-Solution Approach

Is there something wrong with your tuition aid program? Then tell your audience about the problem and propose some solutions.

Do this with candor and honesty. If you have a problem, bring it out into the open. Chances are, your audience *already* knows about the problem. Admit it honestly, and you'll come across as credible.

Also, if you think your proposed solutions will be difficult, say so. No one likes a snow job.

Geographical Order

Organizing a national sales conference? Start by reporting sales in the eastern districts and work west.

Reviewing the physical expenditures of your company's plants? Start with the northern ones and work south.

Evaluating the productivity of your bank's branches? Take it neighborhood by neighborhood.

Alphabetical Order

Why not? This certainly is easy for the audience to follow. And there are times when alphabetical order may be the only way to organize your information—lists of committees or departments, for example.

Psychological Order

Sometimes it's best to organize your speech based on the psychological needs of the audience.

What will they find most acceptable? Most important? Most interesting? Put that first.

Think about the attitudes your audience may have. If you expect them to be hostile or resistant, then ease slowly into your speech. Begin on common ground and put your most acceptable ideas up front. Don't expect to convince everyone of everything. There's usually a limit to the controversial ideas that any audience can accept.

Dr. Robert Klaus, chairman of Columbia University's psychology department, says, "If the opinion you express differs by more than a certain margin from those to whom you're speaking, you'll probably have no effect on them at all." To illustrate his point, he notes that a pro-abortion speaker would have a very small impact on a Right-to-Life audience, regardless of the quality of the speaker's argument.

Some sensitive areas in the business world (pro/anti nuclear power and labor/management confrontations, for example) *require* attention to psychological order.

Transitions

No matter which method you use, make sure you follow the order *smoothly.* Do not get sidetracked. If you say something like, "But before I do that, I'd like to give you a little background on the history of our firm," you're heading for trouble.

Keep things moving. Use strong transitions to help the audience follow your ideas. Try such transitional phrases as:

- Moving on to the second territory . . .
- Now let's take a look at . . .
- So much for supply, but what about demand?
- Switching now to the western division . . .
- Looking ahead to the next five years . . .
- Now let me shift gears for a moment . . .
- But to look at it another way . . .
- In addition . . .

Special Circumstances

How to Handle a Crisis

Your company faces a serious crisis, and it's your job to explain the issue to the employees.

1st: Present several undeniable facts that show the seriousness of the situation. Do this *up front.* Be sure to do it without exaggeration, or the audience will suspect your motives.

2nd: Explore possible solutions to the crisis: tighter budget control, increased productivity, etc.

3rd: Solicit the ideas and support of *everyone* in the company to make the program work. Let them know exactly what you expect from them.

Caution: Don't treat every situation like a crisis, or you will lose credibility. You are entitled to one, maybe two, crises in your career. No more.

If you try to turn every situation into a crisis, your audience will see you as the little boy who cried wolf once too often. They won't bother to listen anymore.

How to Express Disappointment

Suppose some big plan failed—and failed publicly. Now it's your responsibility to tell the audience why the old plan failed and to make some new proposals.

Beware. The audience may be extremely sensitive about the issue and they may fear being blamed for the whole mess.

Reassure them that the original plan was a good one. Say it made sense based on the information available at the time it was conceived. Say no one could have predicted the sudden changes in events that caused the original plan to fail.

Once the audience feels safe from any finger-pointing, they will be receptive to your message.

State the problem clearly and objectively. Admit disappointment, but don't dwell on past failures. Let your emphasis be on a new plan that's based on new data.

How to Turn a Negative Into a Positive

Did your fund-raising campaign fail to meet its goals? Then find a way to turn those negative facts into a positive truth.

Here is how Robert W. Scherer, chairman and CEO of the Georgia Power Company, handled an under-target United Way campaign:

> Our sights were set high this year—higher than some of us thought it would be possible to reach. We set a campaign goal of almost $25 million.
>
> We didn't raise 100 percent of that rather high goal. But we came within an eyelash. We raised 98 and a half percent. . . .
>
> In fact, we raised $2.5 million more than had been raised in the previous campaign. In my book, that's a tremendous accomplishment.

As Frank Lloyd Wright put it, "The truth is more important than the facts." If some of your facts are disappointing, try to find a larger, more positive truth.

One Final Point

Double-check your speech to make sure that if you say "first," you follow it with a "second." Otherwise your audience—and maybe even you—will become hopelessly lost.

Be careful, though, not to overuse the "first, second, third" references. They can be boring.

TELL THEM WHAT YOU TOLD THEM: THE CONCLUSION

Now's the time to sum it up—simply and directly. No new thoughts, please. You must avoid the temptation to "stick in" any additional points at the end. It's too late for that.

Your conclusion may be the only thing the audience remembers, so make it memorable.

Here are some effective ways to end a speech:

End with a Quotation

Walter Wriston, chairman of Citibank/Citicorp, ended his speech to the American Council of Life Insurance with this:

> Sometimes the nonexpert says it best. Gertrude Stein was certainly not an expert in finance, but she understood better than anyone what I have been trying to say. "The money is always there, but the pockets change; it is not in the same pockets after a change; and that is all there is to say about money."
>
> If the consumer has his or her way, there is going to be a lot of pocket-changing.

Refer to the Opening of Your Speech

From President Ronald Reagan:

> I began these remarks speaking of our children. I want to close on the same theme. Our children should not grow up frightened. They should not fear the future. We're working to make it peaceful and free. . . .
>
> Let us reaffirm America's destiny of goodness and good will. Let us work for peace; and as we do, let us remember the lines of the famous old hymn, "Oh, God of Love, Oh, King of Peace / Make wars throughout the world to cease."

Urge Action

W. Paul Tippett, chairman and CEO of American Motors Corporation, urged his audience—the Rotary Club of Houston—to help get America's basic industries back on track.

> If we don't get serious soon, it may be too late. Without our basic industries, we face a future of second-rate status, politically as well as economically. I don't think that's the America any of us want. But we'll get it if we don't act soon. I urge you to join me in this important endeavor.

End with an Anecdote

Edward Addison, president of the Southern Company, used this closing in a speech to the Alabama Power Speakers' Bureau:

> . . . to anybody who asks what one person can do—I would recall what President Theodore Roosevelt said more than eighty years ago.

The man who had led the Rough Riders—and who won two terms as President—spoke to a Midwestern audience about a crisis then facing the country. When he finished his talk, a member of the audience came up to Roosevelt and said, "Mr. President, I'm just an ordinary businessman. What can I possibly do to help?"

And Teddy Roosevelt replied, "Do what you can—with what you've got—where you are. But do it!"

Be Realistic

U.S. Congressman Doug Barnard, Jr., spoke realistically about deregulation to the American Bankers Association:

> Finding the solution won't be easy. If there had been any easy answers, we would have found them long ago.
> But it is possible, and together, we *can* do it.
> Not everyone will be a winner. Not everyone will be a loser. But we can all be survivors.

Be Candid and Sincere

William F. Kieschnick, president of Atlantic Richfield Company, made no false promises when he ended his speech to the Western Gerontological Society:

> I don't want to leave you with the impression that business is riding to the rescue, banners flying, cannons booming. It isn't so. No single institution can do that. . . .
> But I do want to say that business seems increasingly ready to work with you. . . .
> We must be patient but nevertheless expectant and, above all, persistent.

End with Optimism

Ted Kennedy closed his concession speech at the 1980 Democratic convention this way:

> For me, a few hours ago, this campaign came to an end. For all those whose cares have been our concern, the work goes on, the cause endures, the hope still lives and the dream shall never die.

End with a Strong Rhetorical Question

Something like this can be effective:
"Can we afford to do it? A more relevant question is, can we afford *not* to?"

End with Words that *Sound* Strong

- "We need to return to that old-fashioned notion of competition—where *substance,* not *subsidies,* determines the winner." This ending focuses the audience's attention on two contrasting words that begin with the same syllable —*sub.*

- "We worked hard to get this department in tip-top shape. We plan to keep it that way." *Tip-top* repeats the opening and closing consonant sounds.

- "Yes, we ran into some problems. But we corrected them. Perhaps our message should be 'Sighted sub, sank same.' " Good use of alliteration—repetition of initial consonant sounds.

- "Our personnel department's training program works on the premise that 'earning' naturally follows 'learning.' " Rhyme can be catchy, but use it judiciously.

How to Make It Simple

> Except ye utter by the tongue words easy to be
> understood, how shall it be known what is spoken?
> For if not, ye shall speak into the empty air.
> —St. Paul

Speeches are meant to be heard, not read. That means you have to keep your language simple and easily understood. Write for the ear, not the eye.

Remember: Your audience will have only one shot to get your message. They can't go back and re-read a section that's fuzzy, as they can with a book or a newspaper article. Get rid of any fuzzy parts *before* you give the speech.

Never be content with your first draft. *Never.* After you've written it, read it aloud.

Let some time elapse between your rewrites. Let the whole thing sit overnight or over a couple of nights, if possible. Then go at it with a red pen. Cut ruthlessly. Simplify your language.

This chapter will show you—in step-by-step detail—how to simplify the language in your speech. It will help you:

- choose the right word
- simplify your phrases
- sharpen your sentences

CHOOSE THE RIGHT WORD

How can you choose the right words for your speech?
Use these guidelines for starters:

Never Use a Long Word When a Short One Will Do

Mark Twain once said, "By hard, honest labor, I've dug all the large words out of my vocabulary . . . I never write *metropolis* for seven cents because I can get the same price for *city.* I never write *policeman* because I can get the same price for *cop.*"

That's pretty good advice—even if you aren't getting paid by the word. Count the number of syllables in your words. If most of your words have three, four, or (God forbid) five syllables, your writing will be too weak to impress your audience. Find shorter words to get your ideas across.

Consider these two examples of strong speechwriting:

Winston Churchill: "Give us the tools and we will do the job."

Nelson Rockefeller: "In 1960, they said I dropped out too soon. In 1964, they said I hung in too long. So, this year, I played it safe. I did both."

Powerful, memorable statements, right? Notice that they were both written with one-syllable words.

Of course, you can't write a speech *entirely* with one-syllable words (although that might be something to aspire to). But, you should always re-read your first draft and look for words to make shorter and stronger.

That's what Franklin Delano Roosevelt did when his speechwriter gave him this weak sentence: "We are endeavoring to construct a more inclusive society." FDR said the same thing much more powerfully by getting rid of the three- and four-syllable words and using shorter ones. This is his rewrite: "We are going to make a country in which no one is left out."

Use the following list to make your own substitutions:

Instead of	Try using
abbreviate	shorten
accommodate	serve
advise	tell
aggregate	total, whole
anticipate	expect
approximately	about
ascertain	find out, figure out
burgeoning	growing
cessation	end
cognizant	aware
commencement	start, beginning
compel	make
component	part
conjecture	guess
currently	now
deceased	dead
demonstrate	show
desire	want
determine	find out
diminutive	little
discourse	talk
disseminate	spread
duplicate	copy
eliminate	cut out
elucidate	clarify
encounter	meet
endeavor	try
engage	hire
eradicate	wipe out
execute	do
expedite	speed

Instead of	Try using
expire	die
facilitate	make easy
feasible	possible
forward	send
generate	make, cause
heretofore	until now
illustrate	show
indicate	say
initial	first
inquire	ask
locate	find
maintenance	upkeep
marginal	small
numerous	many
observe	see, watch
obtain	get
operate	work, use
originated	began
peruse	read
precipitate	cause
presently	soon
procure	get, take
recapitulate	sum up
recess	break
render	give, send
remunerate	pay
represents	is
require	need
reside	live
residence	home
retain	keep
review	check
saturate	soak

Instead of	*Try using*
solicit	ask
stated	said
stringent	strict
submit	send
subsequent	next
substantial	large
sufficient	enough
supply	send
terminate	end
utilize	use
vacate	leave
vehicle	truck, car, van, bus
verification	proof

A final point: The Gettysburg Address is one of the world's most memorable speeches. Lincoln wrote 76 percent of it with words of *five letters or less.* Consider that an inspiration for you to do the same.

Avoid Jargon

Jargon doesn't work in a speech. It smacks of "bureaucratese" and audiences tend to block it out. It may even alienate some listeners. Get rid of it.

Jargon	*Plain English*
conceptualize	imagine
finalize	finish, complete
a guesstimate	a rough estimate
impact (verb)	affect
implement	carry out
infrastructure	foundation, framework

Jargon	*Plain English*
interface (verb)	talk with
meaningful	real
operational	okay, working
optimum	best
output	results
parameters	limits
utilization	use
viable	workable

Avoid Euphemisms

Euphemisms "bloat" a speech. Replace them with plain English.

Euphemism	*Plain English*
classification device	test
disadvantaged	poor
interrelated collectivity	group
inventory shrinkage	theft
motivational deprivation	laziness
negative patient care outcome	death
nomenclature	name
passed away	died
terminated	fired
unlawful or arbitrary deprivation of life	murder
unscheduled intensified repairs	emergency repairs

Avoid Vague Modifiers

Words such as "very," "slightly," and "extremely" are too vague to be useful. Use words or phrases that say *precisely* what you mean.

Vague	*Specific*
The personnel department is rather understaffed, but the situation will be corrected in the very near future.	The personnel department now has three vacancies. We will fill these jobs within the next month.

Don't Speak in Abbreviations

You may know what HEW, SEC, and FCC stand for, but don't assume that everyone else does.

You have to explain every abbreviation you use—not *every* time you use it, but at least the *first* time.

The same goes with acronyms, such as NOW for the National Organization for Women and PAC for political action committee. Unlike those abbreviations that are pronounced letter by letter (HEW, SEC, FCC, for example), acronyms are pronounced like words. You can use them in a speech, but be sure to identify them the first time.

Don't Speak in Foreign Languages

If you're addressing an English-speaking audience, why would you want to throw in foreign phrases? To show the audience how educated you are? To impress them with your sophistication? To display a bit of class?

Forget it.

Not everyone in your audience will know the meaning of

pro bono publico, Wanderjahr, or *chateaux en Espagne.* For that matter, you may not even know how to pronounce them properly, and that will make you appear foolish to the more knowledgeable members of your audience.

If you want to use a foreign proverb to illustrate a point, translate it into English. For example: "The French have a wonderful saying, 'The more things change, the more they stay the same.' This sentiment certainly describes our organization. We've served this community for fifty years. We've changed our structure along the way, but we haven't changed our goals."

Avoid Sexist Language

There are several ways to avoid sexist implications in your speech.

Find substitutes for compound nouns that contain **man** *or* **woman.** This list should help:

businessmen	business people
cleaning woman	office cleaner
Congressmen	members of Congress
firemen	fire fighters
foreman	supervisor
insurance salesman	insurance agent
mailmen	mail carriers
man-hours	worker-hours
man's achievements	human achievements
mankind	human beings
manpower	labor force
policeman	police officer
political man	political behavior
salesmen	sales representatives, sales clerks, sales force

social man	society
statesman	leader

Shift to the plural.

Before	After
When a *manager* goes on a business trip, *he* should save all of *his* receipts.	When *managers* go on business trips, *they* should save all of *their* receipts.
A utility tax hits the *consumer* where *he* is already overburdened.	A utility tax hits *consumers* where *they* are already overburdened.

Restructure the sentence.

Before	After
The company will select someone from the Treasury Department *to be chairman* of the Travel and Entertainment Committee.	The company will select someone from the Treasury Department *to head* the Travel and Entertainment Committee.

Alternate male and female examples.

Before	After
Interviewers are too quick to say, *"He* doesn't have enough technical knowledge," or *"He's* just not the right *man* for us."	Interviewers are too quick to say, *"He* doesn't have enough technical knowledge," or *"She's* just not the right *person* for us."

Be sure that you don't always mention the male first. Switch the order: husbands and wives, hers or his, him or her, women and men.

Avoid male/female stereotypes.   Doctors, nurses, and even astronauts come in both sexes. *Do not* refer to someone as a "female doctor" or a "male nurse." It's gratuitous.

SIMPLIFY YOUR PHRASES

A phrase with too many words becomes meaningless.

Look at your draft, and get rid of pompous, wordy, and overwritten constructions. Use the following list as a guideline:

Instead of	*Try using*
a large number of	many
a sufficient number of	enough
a total of 42	42
advance planning	planning
are in agreement with	agree
as indicated in the following chart	the following chart shows
as you know	*Delete* (If they already know, why tell them?)
at that point in time	then
at the present time	now
at the time of presenting this speech	today
basically unaware of	did not know
be that as it may	but
blame it on	blame
both alike	alike
brief in duration	short
bring the matter to the attention of	tell
caused damage to	damaged
check into the facts	check the facts

Instead of	Try using
consensus of opinion	consensus
continue on	continue
curiously enough	curiously
demonstrate the ability to	can
despite the fact that	although
due to the fact that	because
end product	product
equally as	equally
estimated at about	estimated at
exert a leadership role	lead
firm commitment	commitment
for free	free
for the purpose of	for
frame of reference	viewpoint, perspective
give encouragement to	encourage
have a discussion	discuss
hold a meeting	meet
hold in abeyance	suspend
in the majority of instances	most often, usually
in the area of	approximately
in connection with	on, of
in close proximity	near
in view of	because
in the event of	if
in the vicinity of	near
in order to	to
in many cases	often
in some cases	sometimes
in the course of	during
individuals who will participate	participants
is of the opinion that	thinks
is in an operational state	operates, works

Instead of	*Try using*
is equipped with	has
is noted to have	has
it is recognized that	*Delete*
it is recommended by me that	I recommend
it has been shown that	*Delete*
it may be mentioned that	*Delete*
join together	join (unless in a marriage ceremony, where "join together" is acceptable)
made a complete reversal	reversed
make a decision	decide
my personal opinion	my opinion
needless to say	*Delete* (If you don't *need* to say it, why *would* you say it?)
new innovations	innovations
newly created	new
never before in the past	never
obtain an estimate of	estimate
of sufficient magnitude	big enough
off of	off
on a national basis	nationally
on the basis of	from
on the occasion of	when
optimum utilization	best use
over with	over
past experience	experience
personal friend	friend
predicated on	based on
prior to	before
provide assistance to	help
start off	start

Instead of	*Try using*
study in depth	study
subsequent to	after
take action	act
the major portion	most
the reason why is that	because
until such time as	until
very unique	unique
was in communication with	talked with
with reference to	about
with the result that	so that
with regard to	about
with the exception of	except
would invoke an expenditure of approximately	would cost about

If your speech is filled with statements such as "This has been a most challenging year," or "We all face a golden opportunity," or "We will meet our challenges with optimism and view the future with confidence," it is probably high on fluff and low on content. Unfortunately, too many business speeches fall into this category.

To get rid of fluff, try this experiment. Listen to ten ordinary business speeches and count the number of times words such as "challenge" and "opportunity" are used. Pay careful attention to the opening and closing sections of the speeches, because that's where amateur writers tend to throw in the most fluff.

Then, listen to ten speeches that you can assume to be "ghostwritten"—speeches, for example, that are given by the President of the United States. These speeches will have fewer "challenges" and "opportunities" in their texts. Why? Because professional speechwriters try to avoid such fluff. They know that audiences block it out.

Follow the professionals. Review your speech and get rid of any glib expressions. If you want your message to stand out, put content—not fluff—into your speech.

SHARPEN YOUR SENTENCES

There are several important things to know about sentences.

Short sentences are stronger than long sentences.

Try this experiment: Take a sample page from your draft and count the number of words in each sentence. Write the numbers down and average them.

If you average twenty or more words per sentence, you'd better start cutting. Why? Because an audience can't follow what you're saying if you put too many words in a sentence. Your message just gets lost.

If you don't believe me, read your longest sentence aloud, then read your shortest sentence aloud. See which one is more powerful—and more memorable.

Variety is the spice of life.

If all your sentences are long, no one will be able to follow you. But if all your sentences are short, your speech may become boring. People get tired of hearing the same rhythm. If you use a rather long sentence, precede or follow it with a short, punchy one. The contrast will catch your audience's attention.

FDR was a master of this technique, and his speeches show a great sense of rhythm and timing. Consider the following example. He uses a powerful, two-word sentence followed by a rhythmic, eighteen-word sentence:

> Hostilities exist. There is no mincing the fact that our people, our territory and our interests are in grave danger.

Ronald Reagan also knew how to vary the rhythm of his speech:

> Everyone is against protectionism in the abstract. That is easy. It is another matter to make the hard, courageous choices when it is your industry or your business that appears to be hurt by foreign competition. I know. We in the United States deal with the problem of protectionism every day of the year.

Count the words he used: seven in the first sentence, then three, then twenty-six, then two, then sixteen. Average length? About eleven words per sentence.

Use the active, not the passive, voice.

It's time for a grammar lesson. I'll keep it brief.

These sentences are in the *active voice* because they show that the subject acts, or does something:

> The Customer Inquiry Department *answers* almost four hundred phone calls every day.
>
> Our new maintenance program *saved* the company $5,000 in the first six months.
>
> The committee *records* all suggestions in a log book.
>
> Government *must place* some constraints on these contracts to prevent price excesses.

A sentence is in the *passive voice* when the subject is acted upon:

> Almost four hundred phone calls *are answered* by the Customer Inquiry Department every day.
>
> $5,000 *was saved* by the company in the first six months of our new maintenance program.
>
> All suggestions *are recorded* by the committee in a log book.

Some constraints *must be placed* on these contracts by government to prevent price excesses.

Read the above sentences aloud, and notice that the active voice:

1. sounds more vigorous
2. is more personal
3. uses fewer words
4. is easier to follow
5. is easier to remember

Get rid of passive constructions in your speech. They sound stilted, flat, and contrived.

Cut "I think," "I believe," "I know," "It seems to me that," "In my opinion."

These expressions weaken sentences. Cut them, and you will make your sentences stronger.

Before	*After*
We think prices are already too high and we know people are hurting.	Prices are already too high and people are hurting.

Avoid "There are."

Sentences that begin with "There are . . ." are often weak. Try rewriting them.

Before	*After*
There are alternative ways that must be found by us to solve the problem.	We must find other ways to solve the problem.

Beware of tongue twisters.

Read your speech aloud several times, and listen carefully for potential tongue twisters.

Try to round up a couple of junior high youngsters and have them listen to your speech. They are notorious for spotting potential tongue twisters, especially those that sound obscene. Better to have some junior high kids spot an embarrassing phrase than to have your audience laugh at it.

A final bit of advice from George Orwell on how to make your writing simple:

1. Never use a long word where a short one will do.
2. If it is possible to cut out a word, always cut it out.
3. Never use the passive where you can use the active.
4. Never use a foreign phrase, a scientific word, or a jargon word if you can think of an everyday English equivalent.
5. Break any of these rules sooner than say anything barbarous.

Style

> If you have an important point to make, don't try to be
> subtle or clever. Use a pile driver. Hit the point once.
> Then come back and hit it again. Then hit it a third
> time—a tremendous whack.
>
> —Winston Churchill

Business executives, politicians, and civic leaders give thousands of speeches every day. Most of these speeches are forgotten as soon as the audience leaves the room—if not sooner.

But, some speeches *do* linger in the minds and hearts of audiences. What makes these speeches special? Style.

Speeches with style have a certain "ring" that makes them *easy* to remember. They have a psychological appeal that makes them seem *important* to remember. And they create an impact that makes them irresistibly *quotable*.

Here are some techniques that professional speechwriters use.

HOW TO USE TRIPARTITE DIVISION

Tripartite division is a device that breaks things into three parts. Three has always been a powerful number. Consider:

- the Holy Trinity
- the three wise men and their three gifts

- God's three attributes: omniscience, omnipotence, and omnipresence
- Goldilocks and the three bears
- the scientific method: hypothesis, inference, and verification
- in baseball: Three strikes and you're out!
- from the battlefield: Ready! Aim! Fire!

For some mysterious reason, the human mind is strongly attracted to things that come in "three's." You can make this attraction work for you by using tripartite division in speeches. Throughout history, speakers have known that tripartite division is a powerful mnemonic device.

- *Julius Caesar:*   "Veni, vidi, vici."

- *Abraham Lincoln:*   "We cannot dedicate, we cannot consecrate, we cannot hallow this ground."

- *Franklin Delano Roosevelt:*   "I see one-third of a national ill-housed, ill-clad, ill-nourished."

- *Ronald Reagan:*   "We will never compromise our principles and standards. We will never give away our freedom. We will never abandon our belief in God."

Admittedly these are some of the biggest names of history. But we ordinary people can make tripartite division work to our advantage, too.

- *a department manager:*   "We need to develop guidelines, establish controls, and set limits."

- *a civic leader:*   "The promise is there, the logic is overwhelming, the need is great."

- *the recipient of an award for community service:*   "My volunteer work has been my life, my inspiration, my joy."

- *a bank manager:* "We do not wield the power we once did—power over our employees, our customers, our communities."

HOW TO USE PARALLELISM

Use a parallel structure to create balance—the emotional appeal of harmony.

- *John Fitzgerald Kennedy:* "If a free society cannot help the many who are poor, it cannot save the few who are rich."

- *Richard Nixon:* "Where peace is unknown, make it welcome; where peace is fragile, make it strong; where peace is temporary, make it permanent."

- *St. Francis of Assisi:* "Lord, make me an instrument of Your peace; where there is hatred, let me sow love; where there is injury, pardon; where there is discord, union; where there is doubt, faith; where there is despair, hope; where there is darkness, light; and where there is sadness, joy."

- *a steel executive:* "We must analyze the problem, then we must find the solution."

- *an honoree:* "And, as we rediscover our priorities, let us rediscover our humanity."

- *a college president:* "We expect to be around for a long time, and we expect to remain strong for a long time."

HOW TO USE IMAGERY

Be specific, be vivid, be colorful . . . and you will make your point. Even better, your audience will *remember* your point.

- *Winston Churchill:* "An iron curtain has descended across the continent."
- *Franklin Delano Roosevelt:* "When you see a rattlesnake poised to strike, you do not wait until he has struck before you crush him."

Again, you don't have to be a famous politician to come up with powerful imagery. Smart business people do it all the time:

- *Richard J. Ferris, CEO of United Airlines:* "As you know, United virtually stood alone in the airline industry as a supporter of deregulation. For a while, at industry meetings, I was about as popular as a skunk at a lawn party."

HOW TO USE INVERSION OF ELEMENTS

If you switch the elements in paired statements, you can produce some memorable lines.

- *John Fitzgerald Kennedy:* "Ask not what your country can do for you. Ask what you can do for your country."
- *a store owner:* "We would rather be a big fish in a small pond than a small fish in a big pond."

HOW TO USE REPETITION

Audiences do not always pay attention. Their minds wander. They think about the work that's piled up on their desks. They think about the bills that are piled up at home. They often miss whole sections of a speech.

If you have an important word or phrase or sentence, be

sure to repeat it. Again. And again. Jesse Jackson knew how to use this technique in his campaign speeches for the presidential nomination: "We must give peace a chance. We must give peace a chance. We must, we must!"

EIGHT

Humor: What Works, What Doesn't, and Why

If you can't be funny, be interesting.
—Harold Ross, founder of *The New Yorker*

Some people think they absolutely must use a joke to begin a speech. I hope you are not one of these people.

Jokes can be risky. There's nothing worse than a joke that falls flat—unless it's a joke that falls flat at the beginning of a speech. Beware.

Ask yourself five questions before you plan to use a joke *anywhere* in your speech:

- "Will this joke tie into the subject and mood of my speech?"
- "Will my audience feel comfortable with this joke?"
- "Is the joke short and uncomplicated?"
- "Is the joke fresh?"
- "Can I deliver this joke really well—with confidence and ease and perfect timing?"

If you can't answer "yes" to all of these questions, scrap the joke.

USING A LIGHT TOUCH

Professional comedians like jokes that produce loud laughs. But you are a speaker, not a professional comedian.

Don't focus on jokes that beg for loud laughs because this usually backfires. Instead, try to develop a "light touch" of humor. You can do this through:

- personal anecdotes
- one-liners that blend into the speech
- humorous quotations
- quips that seem off-the-cuff (but are actually planned)
- clever statistics
- careful choice of words
- gestures
- voice intonations
- smiling

Using a light touch of humor will help the audience to see you as a decent, humane, friendly person. It will help put the audience in a receptive mood for the message of your speech.

WHAT WORKS

What kind of humor works best in a speech? The kind that is friendly and personal and natural. Humor in a speech doesn't need to produce guffaws. A few smiles and some chuckles are just fine for your purpose.

Where can you find this humor? Many speakers buy books of jokes and adapt the material to suit their own needs. These sources can be helpful, but *only* if you use them judiciously. *Don't* use the material verbatim. Always adapt the humor to your own needs and your own style.

Learn to create *your own* light touches of humor. Original

material will work better than material that is lifted straight from books.

Why? Three big reasons:

1. If you create your own humorous touches, you can be sure this material will be fresh to your audience.

2. If the humor comes from your own experience, you will deliver it more naturally and more effectively.

3. If you share something personal with the audience, they will feel more friendly toward you.

Your safest bet for good humor in a speech is to poke gentle fun at yourself. Try making light of:

- *Your personality.* When Senator John Glenn spoke at the Gridiron Dinner in Washington, he mocked his reputation for being dull: "I am not dull. Boring, maybe, but not dull."

- *Your fame.* A little boy once asked John F. Kennedy how he became a war hero. "It was absolutely involuntary," Kennedy replied. "They sank my boat."

- *Your hard-to-pronounce name.* Leo Buscaglia, educator and author of *Living, Loving and Learning,* often begins his speeches with a funny story about his unpronounce-able name:

I am overwhelmed at the pleasure of being introduced by some-one who knows how to pronounce my name. I love to talk about my name because it's one of those beautiful Italian names that has every letter in the alphabet. It's spelled B-u-s-c-a-g-l-i-a, and it's pronounced like everything. The best thing, I think, that has ever happened with it in terms of introductions was when I was making a long distance telephone call. The line was busy and the operator said she'd call me back as soon as the line was free.

When she called back, I picked up the phone and she said, "Would you please tell Dr. Box Car that his telephone call is ready?" I said, "Could that be Buscaglia?" She said, "Sir, it could be damned near anything."

- *Your status.* Before Bishop John J. O'Connor left Scranton, Pennsylvania, to become the Roman Catholic Archbishop of New York, he held a special mass at the University of Scranton. After a solemn procession into the gymnasium, Bishop O'Connor took the microphone and broke the tension with, "I want to remind you, this is not a funeral. Some guys just can't hold a job."

Poking fun at yourself is the safest kind of humor, but never belittle your professional competence in your area of expertise. Otherwise, the audience will wonder why they should bother listening to you.

And never say anything about yourself that you might regret later. A speech is over in fifteen or twenty minutes, but a reputation lasts a lifetime. Don't sacrifice a reputation for a cheap laugh.

OTHER AREAS FOR HUMOR

You can generally make fun of big government, politicians, and high taxes with complete impunity. Audiences *like* to hear speakers make fun of these things; indeed, they often look forward to these digs.

Sex can also be good for a chuckle—providing you don't become sexist. A good example of a workable sex quip comes from Dr. Paul Craig Roberts of Georgetown University: "Reagonomics is kind of like sex. Everybody thinks there is more of it than there really is, and that somebody else is getting most of it."

The following hypothetical quip *wouldn't* work because it smacks of mean sexism: "When my grandfather started this company fifty years ago, doing business was much simpler. But then, again, those were the days when we had only two sexes to deal with."

Of course, you can always get some good mileage out of the weather. Consider this example from David Rockefeller, chairman of Chase Manhattan Bank:

> Coming to Southern California is a delightful way to begin the spring, although your kind invitation might have been even more welcome in the dead of winter. At that time, however, I understand this area was being hit by floods, mud slides, and earth tremors. Somebody probably figured that the last thing you needed was a great gust of wind from the East. I will try to spare you that calamity this afternoon.

WHAT ARE YOUR CHANCES OF GETTING A LAUGH?

You'll find that it's easier to get a laugh as the day goes on. Why? Because it's usually easier to get *anything* as the day goes on.

Early in the morning, people are still groggy. If they think about anything at all, they think about the work that lies ahead of them. They just want to have a cup of coffee and get moving with their schedule. They don't feel much like playing around.

If you're the guest speaker at a breakfast fund raiser, keep everything short and simple. Even if the audience is really interested in your cause, they will be anxious to get out of the meeting and get on with the day's work. No complicated jokes, please.

By lunchtime, things ease up a bit. At least some of the day's work is done, and people can relax with a drink. But, still, they have to get back to the office, and they will be looking at their watches as two o'clock approaches.

By dinner time, things are as loose as they'll ever be. Work is over. People want to put their troubles behind them for a while. They're in the mood to unwind. Indulge them. Give them the chuckles they *want*.

By late evening, however, things may be *too* loose for humor to work. In fact, things may be too loose for *anything* to work. By 10 or 11 o'clock, most audiences are either too drunk or too tired to be receptive to anything.

At this late hour, you must put aside your ego and put aside your prepared speech—no matter how witty or wise that speech might be.

Just give a three- or four-sentence capsule summary of your speech and get the hell out of there. The audience will love you for it.

WHAT ABOUT DELIVERY?

A good delivery will greatly increase your chances of getting a good laugh.

You must be in complete control of the joke or anecdote. You must understand every word, every pause, every nuance. You must—above all—have a good sense of timing.

Want to see how important good delivery is? Practice this fifth-century line from Saint Augustine: "Give me chastity and continence, but not just now." The pause after "continence" makes the whole line.

Don't set yourself up for failure by announcing, "Here's a really funny story." Let the audience decide for themselves if it's really funny or not.

And be prepared in case the audience thinks it *isn't* funny. The only thing worse than the silence that follows a failed joke is the sound of the speaker laughing while the audience sits in embarrassed silence. Don't laugh at your own jokes. As Archie Bunker used to say to Edith, "Stifle yourself."

A FEW WORDS ABOUT SWEARING

Swearing can work in a speech—*if* you know your audience and *if* you choose your words carefully.

When David Brinkley spoke at the annual Chicago Communications luncheon, he included this story about former Vice President Spiro Agnew:

> If I were to go on the air tomorrow night and say "Spiro Agnew is the greatest American statesman since Adams, Hamilton, Jefferson, Washington," the audience would think I'd gone crazy. But Agnew wouldn't. He'd say, "The son of a bitch has finally come to his senses."

David Brinkley knew how to make a point. And you can bet the audience remembered his story.

Just one word about dirty jokes, racial jokes, ethnic jokes, ageist jokes, and sexist jokes:

The word is: *don't.*

Don't use them, *ever.*

These jokes have no place in a business or political speech. If you use them, they will come back to haunt you.

Want proof? Remember Earl Butz.

Want more proof? Remember James Watt.

Special-Occasion Speeches

Not all speeches deal with big issues. Many speeches are simply ceremonial. They honor a person's retirement, or celebrate a college graduation, or dedicate a new building.

These speeches are different from the standard public speech. They're usually much shorter, and they often take a personal approach.

This chapter will give some guidelines on:

- the invocation
- the commencement speech
- the award or tribute speech

It will also help you with some specialized speaking skills:

- how to introduce a speaker
- how to give an impromptu speech
- how to organize a panel presentation
- how to handle a question-and-answer session

THE INVOCATION

The fewer words, the better prayer.
—Martin Luther

The scene: You're sitting on a dais at a banquet. The evening's event? To honor a local business executive with a humanitarian award.

Just before the banquet begins, the master of ceremonies learns that the clergyman who was supposed to offer the invocation can't attend. They need someone to fill in, and they turn to you. "Would you be kind enough to offer grace?"

Well, *would* you? Even more to the point, *could* you?

Could you come up with an invocation that's appropriate for a mixed business gathering—a gathering that might include Catholics, Jews, Protestants, and others?

Avoid prayers that represent a specific religious preference.

A decidedly Protestant prayer, for example, might exclude some parts of the audience. What's worse, it might even *offend* some parts of the audience. I am reminded of an unfortunate invocation that ended with, "We pray for this in Jesus' name." Well, the Jewish man sitting next to me certainly wasn't praying in Jesus' name—and he resented the arrogance of the person who gave that prayer.

Don't give an invocation that might alienate some people in your audience. Instead, come up with something that shows respect for all people—something that honors human dignity.

In a business setting, it's appropriate to:

- give thanks for all blessings
- pray for peace
- ask for wisdom and courage and strength to deal with your problems

Above all, keep it short—under a minute, if you can.

A word of caution about humorous invocations: *don't.* This is not the time to use a light touch. Avoid *anything* such as "Good food, good meat, good God, let's eat." (Yes, I'm told someone actually used that invocation at a civic organization.)

THE COMMENCEMENT SPEECH

Proclaim not all thou knowest.
—Benjamin Franklin

Everyone is in a good mood at a commencement. Students are glad to be finished with exams. Parents are glad to be finished with tuition bills. And instructors are glad to be finished with another academic year.

Don't let long-winded or pompous remarks put them in a bad mood.

Remember: Caps and gowns can be hot. Folding chairs can be uncomfortable. Crowded gymnasiums can be unbearably stuffy. Follow Franklin Delano Roosevelt's advice: "Be brief . . . be sincere . . . be seated."

In the process, of course, try to say something inspirational, thoughtful, encouraging, uplifting, or memorable. The Academy Award–winning actress Meryl Streep knew this when she returned to speak at her alma mater, Vassar College. She encouraged the graduates to strive for excellence, even though life might be difficult at times. "If you can live with the devil," Streep said, "then Vassar has not sunk its teeth into you." This proved to be a great line for a commencement speech—easy for the audience to remember, and irresistible for the press to quote.

It's safest to speak for between ten and fifteen minutes. If you go on longer, the audience may get dangerously restless. After all, a graduating class doesn't have to worry anymore about reprisals from the school principal or the college president. They're free to yawn or talk or even boo. Don't make any remarks about the brevity (or verbosity) of your speech. I once heard a commencement speaker promise to be brief. He was, much to his embarrassment, applauded by a few rambunctious students.

Remember that June weather is notoriously fickle. If the commencement is outdoors, be alert to the storm clouds and be prepared to shorten your address if the rains come.

Also, make sure your hat's on tight. More than one commencement speaker has been embarrassed by a hat flying off into the wind.

THE AWARD OR TRIBUTE SPEECH

> Tis an old maxim in the schools,
> That flattery's the food of fools;
> Yet now and then your men of wit
> Will condescend to take a bit.
> —Jonathan Swift

A person who retires after forty years of service. An employee who contributes a money-saving idea to the company. A telephone installer who saves a customer's life. All of these people deserve some special recognition, and you may be asked to give a speech in honor of one of them.

These five guidelines should help:

1. *Be generous with the praise.*   If one of your employees risked his life to save a customer's life and he's now receiving a special award, you must come up with praise to match the occasion. Be generous.

2. *Be specific.*   Whatever you say should be so specific that it couldn't possibly be said about anyone else. Never, *never* give an award speech that sounds "canned."

For example, if the person is retiring after forty years with the company, mention two or three specific projects he was involved in. Tell how his involvement made a difference.

3. *Be personal.*   Make your tribute reveal a flesh-and-blood person. Show the honoree's personality and vulnerability.

When Senator Ted Kennedy gave a memorial tribute to his brother John, he said of the late President, "He took issues seriously but never himself too seriously. Indeed, his family would not let him. After his election, when we were all at dinner one night, Dad looked at him and then turned to Mother and said with a smile, 'He may be President, but he still comes home and swipes my socks.' "

4. *Be sincere.*   Suppose you must give an award to a person you've never met. Don't pretend to be a close friend or associate. Simply get some information about the person from a supervisor and share this information in a sincere, straightforward way.

For example, "Karen's supervisor has told me how Karen saved a baby's life. I'm glad to meet Karen and to present her with this award for distinguished service. I'm proud to have her as one of our employees."

5. *Be inspirational.*   The Reverend Peter Gomes said this in a memorial tribute to Martin Luther King, Jr., at Harvard University: "We remember Martin Luther King, Jr., not because of his success, but because of our failures; not because of the work he has done, but because of the work we must do."

INTRODUCING A SPEAKER

Your assignment is to introduce a speaker. That's simple. Just
call the speaker and ask for a written introduction—not a resume or a *vita,* but a completely written introduction that you
can deliver.

What a Good Introduction Should Include

A good introduction should be brief—certainly no more than
four minutes, and preferably just a minute or two.
  It should include:

  • several mentions of the speaker's name
  • the speaker's qualifications to talk about the topic
  • the title of the speech

  A good introduction should present this information in a
friendly, personal way. It should *not* sound like a resume. It
should *not* sound like a repetition of the biographical data
already printed on the program.
  If the speaker provides you with a stuffy introduction, rewrite it to sound friendlier. For example, delete a boring list of
professional organizations and fill in with an anecdote that
shows what kind of person the speaker is.
  If the introduction provided is too modest, add some material that shows the speaker's unique qualifications. Quote the
speaker, if possible, or quote someone else's remarks showing
the speaker's special attributes.

Introduction Dos
  • Be sure to pronounce the speaker's name correctly. (Ver-
    ify the pronunciation in advance.)

- Repeat the speaker's name several times during the introduction so the audience can catch it.

- At the end of the introduction, face the audience (*not* the speaker) and announce the speaker's name: "We couldn't have found a more qualified hospital administrator than . . . Peggy Smith."

- Then turn to the speaker and smile.

- In formal situations, applaud until the speaker reaches your side, shake hands, and return to your place.

- In informal situations, sit down as soon as the speaker rises and starts toward the lectern.

- Pay close attention to the speaker's opening. It may contain a reference to you, and you should be prepared to smile or nod in response.

- Plan these movements carefully. Make sure the speaker knows the last line of your introduction so he or she can use it as a cue.

Introduction Don'ts

- Don't upstage the speaker by making your introduction *too* funny. (Let the speaker be the star.)

- Don't try to present a capsule summary of the speaker's speech. (You might misinterpret the speaker's focus, and that would put the speaker at a serious disadvantage.)

- Don't steal the speaker's material. (If the speaker told you a good anecdote over lunch last week, don't use it. The speaker might have planned to use it in the speech.)

- Don't rely on memory. (Write out your introduction in full.)

- Don't ad lib. (Many a "spontaneous" comment has turned into an inane one—especially after a few drinks.)

- Don't draw attention to any negative conditions. (For example, don't say, "We're glad that Josephine has recovered from her heart attack and that she can be with us today." Comments like this do *not* put an audience in a relaxed mood.)

- Don't try to con the audience by saying things such as, "This is the funniest speaker you'll ever hear." (Let the audience make up their own minds.)

- Don't put pressure on the speaker by saying, "Now we'll see whether or not he's an excellent speaker, which I expect he is." (I once heard a CEO make such an introduction, and the speaker looked terrified.)

Seven Cliches That Never Work in an Introduction

These cliches do a disservice to you and to the poor speaker who must follow your introduction. Avoid:

1. "Ladies and gentlemen, here is a speaker who needs no introduction. . . ."
2. "We are truly honored to have with us today . . ."
3. "Without further ado . . ."
4. "It is indeed a high privilege . . ."
5. "On this most memorable and ceremonial occasion . . ."
6. "Ladies and gentlemen, heeeere's . . ."
7. "We are a lucky audience because we have none other than . . ."

I have heard all these introductions used by supposedly intelligent people. I wished I had not, and so did the rest of the audience.

A Tacky Introduction

How many times have you heard someone stand up on a banquet dais and say, "I'd like to introduce Mr. John Jones and his good wife, Nancy"?

What, exactly, is a "good" wife? If John Jones had a "bad" wife, would the host announce that, too?

Get rid of "the good wife" or "the better half." Such phrases are tacky and belittling. Just say, "I'd like to introduce John and Nancy Jones."

And, surely, I don't have to tell you that no one should ever introduce anyone as "the little lady."

THE IMPROMPTU SPEECH

Mark Twain once said, "It takes three weeks to prepare a good ad-lib speech." Alas, he was right. If you're going to a meeting where someone *might* ask you to speak, gather your thoughts in advance.

Ask yourself, "What is likely to happen at this meeting? Who will be there? What will they probably say? Are there any controversial areas? Will people have questions for me? How should I respond?"

Make notes about the topics you think will come up. Practice some impromptus until you are comfortable and convincing. Be sure to practice *aloud.* Your thoughts can't count until they're spoken—and heard.

Perhaps the worst thing that can happen at a meeting is for someone to ask you for an answer/opinion/analysis, and the request catches you totally off guard. You've never given the subject a thought. You don't have any facts or figures. You're in deep trouble, right?

Not necessarily. If you have poise, your audience will forgive you almost anything. Keep your head high, your back straight, your shoulders relaxed, your eyes alert, your voice strong, your pitch moderate.

Above all, don't apologize. Never say anything like, "Oh, I'm so sorry. I feel so embarrassed. I didn't know you'd ask me to speak. I don't have any information with me."

No one expects you to give a keynote address under these circumstances. Just make a comment. If you can't come up with an intelligent response, keep your poise, maintain direct eye contact, and say, in an even voice, "I don't know. I will look into that and get back to you with the information."

How to Organize an Impromptu Speech

- Decide what you want to talk about—*fast!*

- Commit yourself to that approach. Don't change subjects or reverse your opinion midstream.

- Feel free to pause for a few seconds to collect your thoughts. The audience will not think you're stupid; they'll admire you for being able to organize your ideas under difficult circumstances.

- Open with a generalization to stall for time, if necessary. "Deregulation is certainly an important issue right now" will buy you a few extra seconds to compose your response.

- Or, repeat the question to stall for extra time. "You're asking me about the changes that deregulation will bring to the banking industry." Repeating the question has an extra benefit: it makes sure the audience knows what you've been asked to speak about.

- Present just two or three points of evidence. Do not bore the audience with chronological details.

- Wrap up your impromptu speech with a firm conclusion —a punch line that people can focus on.

- Do not ramble. Once you've offered what sounds like a conclusion, just stop.

PANEL PRESENTATIONS

How to Moderate

- Seat the panelists three or four minutes in advance—just long enough to allow them to get their papers in order.

- Make sure they have glasses of water, with extra pitchers on the table. Also make sure they have stopwatches.

- Use large name cards to identify the panelists (by first and last names).

- Start the presentation on time.

- Introduce yourself right away. I once heard a moderator, an editor, ramble on for seventeen minutes before she gave her name. The members of the audience kept whispering to each other, "Who is she? Who is she?" I'm sure they were also wondering, "What's she doing up there?"

- Make sure the audience is comfortable. If people are standing at the back of the room, tell them there are seats available at the front, then pause and allow them to move forward. If you don't take care of these logistics at the beginning, you'll be bothered by rustling noises throughout the panel presentation.

- As you introduce the panelists, use their names two or three times. Unless you are introducing J. D. Salinger, do *not* use initials. Give everyone a first name.

- Tell the purpose of the panel presentation.

- Explain *how* the panel will work (number of minutes allowed for each panelist, time for rebuttals, questions and answers, etc.).

- Give the panelists a "thirty-second signal" so they can wrap up their presentations. One effective technique: simply show the panelist a 3 × 5 card that reads "30 seconds."

- If panelists run overtime, interrupt them—nicely, of course—and give them fifteen seconds to finish.

- *Do not* let any panelist abuse your schedule. Say in a firm, even voice, "Thank you, Mrs. Smith, but your time is up."

- Close the presentation on schedule with a few words of thanks to the panelists and to the audience.

How to Be a Panelist

- Be prepared for the worst. Inexperienced moderators may not know the above guidelines. Try to make the best of the situation.

- If the moderator forgot name cards or didn't pronounce your name properly, start by saying, "Hello. I'm *(name).*"

- If the moderator didn't give you an adequate introduction, briefly give your credentials and explain why you're there.

- If you are the last speaker and the time has run out, know how to give a shortened presentation.

- If another panelist refuses to stop speaking and the moderator can't control the situation, you may be forced to assert yourself. Take heart from Maxine Waters, the state legislator from Los Angeles. When Senator Gary Hart was trying to woo delegates to the National Women's Political Caucus convention in San Antonio, he supposedly ignored five warnings that his time was up. Maxine Waters, one of the panelists, finally demanded, "What does your refusal to relinquish the podium say about your attitude toward women?" What, indeed?

QUESTION-AND-ANSWER SESSIONS

I've always followed my father's advice. He told me, first, to always keep my word and, second, to never insult anybody unintentionally. If I insult you, you can be goddamn sure I intend to.
—John Wayne

A question-and-answer session can make or break your speech. Plan to make the Q&A work *for* you, not *against* you.

You should prepare for a Q&A as carefully as you prepare for a speech. Always develop a list of possible questions. Be realistic. If you're giving a speech on a controversial topic, you can expect to receive some tough questions.

Consult with the people in your business who work close to the news—for example, the consumer advocate, the treasurer, the public relations staff. Have them review your list of possible questions. Ask them to add to it.

Don't be intimidated by the difficulty of these questions. Don't allow yourself to be placed in a defensive position. Instead, come up with answers that work to *your* advantage. Practice these answers—*aloud.* It doesn't do any good to plan an assertive response if you can't sound assertive when you give it.

Here are ten practical tips to help you with a question-and-answer session:

1. *Take questions from all parts of the audience.*

2. *Listen carefully to each question.* Don't smile or frown excessively as you listen—save your response until it's time for you to answer. And don't nod your head enthusiastically to show you understand the question. The audience may think you automatically agree with the question.

3. *Pay attention to your posture and body language.* Avoid any fidgeting motions that might reveal anxiety. Never, for example, light up a cigarette while you are being asked a question.

4. *Treat every questioner as an equal.* Don't try to compliment someone by saying, "Good question." It implies the others were *not* good questions. Be especially careful not to "brush off" questions from your subordinates or to fawn over comments from your superiors.

5. *Repeat all positive questions.* This makes sure the audience has heard the question. It also buys you a few seconds of time to prepare your response.

6. *Paraphrase the negative questions.* This allows you to set the tone and to control the emphasis of your answer. *Don't* repeat any hostile language, e.g., "Why did we fire all the older workers who had been with the company for so many years?" If you repeat it, you might be quoted as actually saying it.

7. *Look first at the person who asked the question.* Then establish good eye contact with the whole audience as you give the answer.

8. *Respond simply and directly.* If your response is too long, the audience may think you're trying to stall for time to avoid further questions.

9. *Don't extend your answers.* The more you say, the more chance you have to hang yourself. Remember Calvin Coolidge: "I have never been hurt by anything I didn't say."

10. *Don't limit yourself by saying, "This will be our last question."* If that question turns out to be a difficult one and you handle it poorly, you will end in a needlessly weak position. Instead, try saying, "We have a few minutes left. Can I take another question?" If you feel confident with the answer you give, then let this be the last question and wrap up the session. If you aren't satisfied to end the session at this point, you still have the option of accepting another question.

How to Handle Special Problems in a Q&A Session

• *If no one asks you a question.* Don't just stand there in silence. Ask yourself a question. Try, "Last week, when I spoke to the Chamber of Commerce, several people asked me about our plans to build a new plant. Perhaps I should spend a few minutes on that."

• *If someone asks about something you already discussed in the speech.* Answer anyway. Perhaps you didn't make your message clear enough. Try another approach. If you used an anecdote to explain something during your speech, use statistics or quotations to clarify the point during your Q&A. If the audience didn't understand your first technique, maybe they'll understand your second or third.

- *If someone repeats a question that's already been asked.* Don't answer it again. "I believe we've already answered that" will usually work.

- *If someone tries to turn a question into a long-winded speech.* Stop him or her politely but firmly. Interrupt the person's rambling and ask him or her to come to the point and give the question—"in the interest of saving time." The rest of the audience will appreciate this indication that you value their time. Gestures can help. When you interrupt the questioner, raise your hand in front of you. This "stop sign" signal will reinforce your words.

- *If someone asks a totally irrelevant question (perhaps about your personal life).* Just say, "Well, that's not what we're here to discuss." Period. End of discussion.

- *If someone asks a disorganized question.* Respond to only one part and ignore the rest. Naturally, pick the part of the question that will help you to reinforce your message.

- *If you don't know the answer.* Say so. Offer to get the information and send it to the person.

- *If you run out of time.* Say you're sorry you couldn't get to answer every question. Offer to make yourself available to people who want to pursue the subject further—perhaps during a coffee break or during a cocktail hour.

How to Respond to Hostile Questions

You're the manager of consumer conservation at an electric utility, and you've just finished speaking to a community group about energy-saving ideas. Up pops a hand, and you hear this question: "How can you stand there and talk about conservation when thousands of old people in your service area are so poor that they can't even eat? What do you want them to do? Pay high rates and eat cat food?"

How do you get out of this one? Very carefully.

Hostile questions are *not* impossible to answer. They just require special skills. Learn the techniques and practice them. Do it now, before you need to use these skills. Don't wait until you're put on the spot. It's too late then.

Start by giving yourself three basic rights:

- the right to be treated fairly
- the right to stay in control—of yourself and the situation
- the right to get your message across correctly

Remember: You are the invited speaker. No one in the audience has the right to take your role or to obscure your message.

Concentrate on getting your message across. In preparation for any Q&A, choose two or three important points that you can express as one-liners. Memorize these lines. Use them as *focus statements* when the Q&A gets difficult.

Rephrase any hostile questions so you can get into a *focus statement*.

For example:

Q: "All of your fancy plans to put up these big apartment buildings will just tear up our streets and tear down our old homes. What do you want to do to our downtown area? Kill it?"

A: "You're asking about our redevelopment plans." (rephrased question) *"Well, let me say that we plan to build a healthy downtown—where people can live and where businesses can do business."* (focus statement)

Don't be afraid of hostile questions. As Edmund Burke put it: "He who opposes me, and does not destroy me, strengthens me."

It's also imperative that you never insult anyone. "Well, I'd never insult anyone in a question-and-answer session. That would be mean. And dangerous." Is this what you're thinking to yourself?

You're right. It *would* be mean and dangerous to insult anyone during a Q&A. But unthinking speakers do it all the time. Let me share a few bad examples so you can learn from their lessons.

> *Q:* "Why is the company authorizing so much stock? That's way too much!"
> *A:* "Do you know the difference between issued and authorized stock? Issued stock is . . ."
> *Q:* "Are you saying I don't know what I'm talking about!"

Don't accidentally insult a questioner's intelligence. Listen respectfully to the question, then try, "For the benefit of the whole audience, let me explain the difference between *issued* and *authorized* stock."

> *Q:* "Why didn't you do more testing on that drug before you sold it to the public?"
> *A:* "If you'd been listening to my speech, you'd obviously know the answer to that question."

Don't embarrass questioners in public. They will never forget the humiliation, and they will hold it against you.

Warning: "Obviously" can be an emotionally charged word. It often seems like a put-down. After all, if something was so obvious, why did the questioner miss it? Is he or she stupid?

A heckler dominated the Q&A session at an important meeting. The speaker grew increasingly frustrated, and finally threatened the heckler with, "I'm going to ask you to sit down in a few minutes."

Of course, the heckler just loved this attention, so he continued to interrupt the Q&A with long-winded questions. Each time, the speaker raised his voice and said, "I'm going to ask you to sit down soon."

Don't make idle threats. The heckler will love the extra attention, and the audience will think you are ineffectual. If you can't carry out a threat, don't make it.

> *Q:* "Why do you think your program is so much better than the one Fred Smith started, which we've been using for years?"
>
> *A:* "Well, there were lots of problems with the old program. For example, . . ."

Don't criticize a predecessor's work. Even if Fred is no longer with the organization, he may have friends and relatives and loyal supporters who still are. They will resent you for knocking his work.

Instead, explain that you inherited a fine structure, but that new information, subsequent events, increased funding, larger staff, or advanced technology allowed you to build on that foundation. For a strong emotional appeal, point out how Fred himself would have probably welcomed the chance to expand his original program: "At Fred's retirement dinner, he said the future seemed to be coming faster and faster—and that he wished he could be around to see all the changes in our industry."

Never give the impression that you've disregarded someone else's work, or the audience will think you are reckless and arrogant.

How to Handle Trick Questions

Questions often fall into patterns. If you recognize the pattern, you can get around the question much better.

Be aware of these trick questions:

- *The "A" or "B" Question.*   "Which is more important to your company—building a new production plant in our town or opening new offices out-of-state?"

   Don't pigeonhole yourself. Say, "They're both important," or "Those are just two of our concerns." Consider this example from a news conference held in Washington, D.C., by Anne McGill Burford, former Administrator of the Environmental Protection Agency:

   Q: "Mrs. Burford, did you jump or were you pushed?"

   A: "I submitted my resignation to the President yesterday afternoon at 5 o'clock."

- *The Multiple Question.*   "Will the university make a special effort to recruit minority students? And will the athletic program be more closely supervised? And will you build any more student housing?"

   Don't get confused by three or four questions at once. Answer only one.

- *The Open Question.*   "Tell me about your company."

   Here is where it pays off to have pre-established *focus statements.* Use them to create the image you want.

- *The "Yes" or "No" Question.*   "Will you have any layoffs next year—yes or no?"

   Never get forced into a yes or no. Make the statement in your own words.

- *The Hypothetical Question.*   "What if the union doesn't accept this offer?"

Avoid being pulled into "doomsday" situations. They're like bottomless pits. Cut off the discussion by saying, "We're confident we'll reach an agreement." Consider this exchange from a news conference with President Reagan:

Q: "Mr. President, if there's no change in the situation, is there a time when you would want to bring the troops home?"

A: "Let me just say that—I got into trouble a little while ago from trying to answer a hypothetical question with a hypothetical answer. And various interpretations were placed on it."

Reagan then avoided a hypothetical answer and gave a *focus statement* that summed up his position.

• *The Off-the-Record Question.* There is no such thing as an off-the-record question in a Q&A session. Answer all questions as though your answer will appear on the front page of tomorrow's paper. It just might!

• *The Ranking Question.* "Would you name the top three concerns of today's teaching profession?"
    Again, don't pigeonhole yourself. As soon as you name the top three concerns, someone will ask, "What's the matter? Don't you care about *(blank)*?" And then you'll be stuck. Instead, try, "Among our most important concerns are . . ."

• *The Non-Question Question.* "I don't think we need all this new equipment."
    How can you respond to such a statement? By converting it into a question. For example: "I'm hearing an important question in your statement, and that question is, 'How can we benefit by using this equipment?' " Then,

you can answer the question without having to rebutt the original statement.

- *The False Premise Question.* "Now that you've dumped all that pollution into the river, how are you going to clean it up?"

  Always correct a false premise. Say in a firm voice, "That's not so. Let me set the record straight."

- *The Cross-Examination Question.* "Let's review the waste disposal issue once again. What possible explanation can you give for this disgraceful situation?"

  If the questioner has unclean motives, address them. Say, "That sounds like a trap. What are you trying to get me to say?" Remember: You are not in a courtroom. You do not have to subject yourself to a cross-examination.

What to Include in Your Answer

- *Cite your own professional experience.* "In my twenty-five years of work in this field, I have never seen anything like that."

- *Cite your own personal experience.* "Well, I just went out and bought a *(blank)*. I know the product's good."

- *Quote the experts.* "The top researchers in the country would disagree with you. At Columbia University, for example, . . ."

- *Present facts.* "The fact of the matter is . . ."

- *Disassociate.* "That's like comparing apples and avocados. We can't be compared."

- *Establish a bond.* "Well, I can certainly understand how you feel. In fact, many people have felt the same way. But when they became more familiar with the program, they found out that . . ."

- *Simplify the numbers.* "Yes, $10,000 *does* seem like a lot of money to spend on training until you consider that this amounts to only 'x' dollars per person. And increased productivity will pay back our initial investment in just one year."

- *Recognize the importance of the question.* Some people don't want an answer. They just want to be heard. They want their day in court. If you recognize this need for attention, you will satisfy them. Play psychologist and say in your most soulful voice, "Sounds like that's an important issue to you." But be careful not to sound patronizing.

- *Above all, include your focus statements.* Use those one-liners that will stick in the minds of the audience—and may be quoted by the press.

How to Use a Bridging Response

Use a *bridging response* when you don't want to discuss the question. Listen to the question, then bridge to one of your focus statements by saying something like this:

- "Well, Paul, the really important issue we should be discussing is . . ."
- "Consumers would be better off if they asked about . . ."
- "That's not the critical issue here. The critical issue is . . ."

In each case, use the bridging response to get into a specific point you want to make.

If possible, address the questioner by name. It produces a calming, persuasive effect.

Use Humor Sparingly—If at All

It's too easy for humor to backfire in a question-and-answer session. Why? Because it seems to be directed at a particular person. If you pick on someone whom the audience really likes, you're in trouble.

For example: "You'd better get to the point of your question because I'm only president of this organization for another eight months." Such a line might draw a laugh, but if you happen to say it to the wrong person, the audience may turn against you.

Of course, there's a flip side to this coin:

If a *questioner* says something funny, chuckle. Show you're human. Never try to top someone's line. Let that person have a brief, shining moment of glory. The audience will appreciate —and respond to—your good-naturedness.

The Nitty-Gritty Details

Let our advance worrying become advance thinking and planning.
—Winston Churchill

Why worry about giving a speech? You'll be much better off if you put your energy into thinking and planning. Think about the logistics of giving your speech. Plan for the unexpected and the unwanted. And prepare, prepare, prepare.

This chapter will show you how to:

- prepare *your speech* for delivery by typing the manuscript in an easy-to-read script format
- prepare *the room* by making the physical layout work for you, not against you
- prepare *yourself* by treating your voice and your body as valuable tools

HOW TO TYPE A SPEECH

Type your speech so that:

- it is easy for you to deliver
- it is easy for the press to read

• it is easy for a substitute speaker to deliver if you are unable to speak

Proper manuscript preparation takes some extra effort, but your efforts will pay off.

Here are twenty-one tips from the professionals:

1. Type the script in *speechwriter*. This is a large-size typeface designed especially for public speakers. Use upper and lower case.

2. If you don't have access to one of these special typewriting elements, just use your regular typewriter and type in all-caps so that the print is large enough for you to see. But be alert: when reading a speech typed with all caps, it is easy to confuse proper nouns with ordinary words.

3. Identify the speech on the top left corner of the first page with:

   YOUR NAME AND TITLE
   THE GROUP YOU'RE SPEAKING TO
   THE CITY YOU'RE SPEAKING IN
   THE DATE OF THE SPEECH

4. Double-space between lines. Triple-space between paragraphs.

5. Start typing the speech about four inches from the top of the first page. This gives you the space to make last-minute additions to your opening.

6. Be sure to end each line with a complete word. *Never* hyphenate words at the ends of lines. Leave the line short rather than hyphenate.

7. Don't break statistics at the end of a line. For example:

   "At our company we spend five
   hundred dollars a week on maintenance."

(When delivering this speech, you might accidentally say "five thousand dollars" and would have to correct yourself.)

8. End each page with a complete paragraph. It's too dangerous to start a sentence on one page and finish it on another. You can lose too much time while shifting the page.

9. Be sure to leave about three inches of white space at the bottom of *each* page. If you try reading copy that runs all the way to the bottom of the page, your head will go too far down, the audience won't be able to see your face, and your volume will decrease.

10. Leave wide margins at the left and right of the copy.

11. Number each page on the upper right.

12. Write out abbreviations (for example, M-B-A) with hyphens.

13. Spell out foreign words and names phonetically. For example, after "Mr. Chianese," write "Mr. Kee-uh-NAY-zee" in parentheses.

14. Don't use roman numerals in the script. They're fine for written presentations, but not speeches. It would sound stilted to say, "now, roman numeral one . . ."

15. Underline words or phrases that are to be emphasized.

16. Use three dots (. . .) to mark slight pauses. They are often useful at the end of a paragraph, to remind you to pause for a second before proceeding.

17. Mark longer pauses with two slash marks (//). These slash marks remind you to stop for a few seconds, either to give the audience time to laugh or to give you time

to change the direction of your speech. If you use slash marks, be sure to drop down a couple of lines before you start typing again.

/ /

Like this. Otherwise, you'll obscure the marks.

18. At the end of the speech, include an address where people can write for more information.

19. Never staple the pages of your speech together. Simply fasten them with a paper clip, which can be easily removed when you're ready to speak.

20. Place the manuscript in a plain, dark folder—ready for your delivery.

21. Always prepare a spare copy and carry it separately. For example, if you're going to deliver an out-of-town speech, carry one copy in your briefcase and another in your suitcase.

HOW TO PREPARE THE ROOM

It's amazing how many good speeches have been ruined by a non-functioning microphone or by miserable lighting or by a poor ventilating system.

You may have prepared a wise and witty speech, but if the audience can't hear you or see you, who cares? And if the audience is suffering from an air-conditioning system that doesn't work, you might as well wrap it up early and head home.

Check out the room before you speak. If you can't go in person, ask someone else to look at it. Or telephone the person who invited you to speak. Ask some basic questions:

- *Does the room have windows?* Even more important, do the windows have heavy drapes? You'll need to close them if you show any slides.

  You'll also need to close the drapes if you're speaking in a motel conference room that looks onto a swimming pool. There's *no way* you can compete with beautiful, firm bodies in scanty bathing wear, so shut those drapes before the audience arrives and save yourself a lot of frustration during the speech.

- *Is there a lectern?* Does it have a light? Is it plugged in and ready to go? Is a spare bulb handy?

  Does the lectern have a shelf underneath where you can keep a glass of water, a handkerchief, a few cough drops?

  Can the lectern be adjusted to the proper height? If you're short, is there a box to stand on? Move everything into place *before* you arrive at the lectern to speak.

- *Can you be heard without a microphone?* If so, don't use one.

- *Is the public address system good?* Test it and ask an assistant to listen to you. Must you stoop or lean to reach the microphone? It should be pointed at your chin. Can you be heard in all corners of the room? Is the volume correct? Do you get feedback? Where do you turn the microphone on and off?

- *How about the lighting?* Do a "test run" with the house lights. Do they create a glare when you look at the audience? In general, the light level on you should be about the same as the light level on the audience. Does a crystal chandelier hanging over your head create a glare for the audience? Remove the bulbs. Will the spotlight appear where it should? Adjust it.

• *What about the seating?* After they've taken off their coats and seated themselves and gotten comfortable, people hate to be asked to move. Perhaps it reminds them of school days. Be sure to arrange the seating to your advantage *before* the audience arrives.

Will people be seated at round dining tables, with some of their backs to you? If so, allow time for them to shuffle their seats before you start to speak.

It's too difficult to maintain eye contact when listeners are scattered around a large room. If you expect a small crowd, try to remove some of the chairs before the audience arrives. Do anything you can to avoid "gaps" in the audience where energy can dissipate.

If you'll speak in a large auditorium, have the rear seats roped off. This forces the audience to sit closer to you. This roped-off area is also great for latecomers. They can slip in without disturbing the rest of the audience.

If only a few people show up, move your lectern from the stage to floor level to create more intimacy. The closer you are to your listeners, and the closer your listeners are to each other, the more successful you will be.

• *Is there good ventilation?* Can the air-conditioning system handle large crowds? Can the heat be regulated?

• *How many doors lead into the room?* Can you lock the doors at the front of the room to prevent intruders from upstaging you? Can you have assistants posted at the rear doors to ensure quiet entrances from latecomers and quiet exits from people who must leave before you finish?

• *Is music being "piped" into the room?* If so, turn it off immediately. Do not rely on hotel staff to do so when it's your time to speak.

• *Is the room soundproof?* This becomes a critical issue when you speak in a hotel room. Who knows what will be happening in the room next to yours: a raucous bachelor party, a pep rally, or an enthusiastic sales pitch. What audience would concentrate on, say, cogeneration if they could listen to the excitement happening next door?

Don't take any chances. If possible, make an unannounced visit to the hotel to check things out for yourself. Hotel managers always say their conference rooms are "nice and quiet." Trust them about as far as you could throw the hotel.

If you find that sound carries through the walls, speak to the manager. Ask to have the adjacent rooms empty during your speech. If the hotel is booked solid, they won't be able to accommodate this request, but it doesn't hurt to ask.

- Above all, get the name and telephone number of a maintenance person who can step right in and replace a fuse or a lightbulb, or adjust the air conditioner. Keep this person's name and number handy at all times.

Emerson was right. *Shallow* men believe in luck.

HOW TO USE AUDIOVISUAL AIDS

More speeches are ruined by audiovisual aids than are improved by them. I caution all speakers to be especially careful here. Don't ruin a first-rate speech with audiovisual materials that are second-rate, or even unnecessary.

A-V aids are unnecessary if they:

- contribute no new information to your speech
- fail to help the audience understand or appreciate your message
- actually *detract* from your role as speaker

Unfortunately, most speakers use audiovisual aids as a "crutch." An all-too-common example:

The speaker says, "I want to tell you about our new accounting system," and then flashes a slide that reads "New Accounting System."

Does this slide contribute any new information? No. Does this slide really help the audience to understand the speaker's message? No. Does this slide detract from the speaker's presence? Unfortunately, yes.

Speeches are designed primarily for the ear, but visuals are designed for the eye. If you are trying to talk while people are looking at visual aids, rather than at you, your words won't be as powerful. Your eye contact with the audience won't be as strong. In short, your message won't be as effective.

Need convincing? Try holding an important conversation on the telephone while looking at a television show. How much information will you miss?

If you really need to use audiovisual aids—to simplify complex information or to create an emotional appeal—use them wisely.

One effective technique is to use an audiovisual "insert." Prepare a short slide show or a videotape and insert this into your speech as a self-contained unit. The audience can concentrate on the audiovisual segment and then return concentration to the remainder of your speech.

Here are some suggestions for effective audiovisual inserts:

Slides

- Set written copy flush left, with a ragged right margin.

- Keep type uniform. Sans-serif type takes enlargement very well. Avoid enlarged typewriter letters.

- Use upper and lower case, not all-capital, letters.

- Use normal spacing between words and caps.

- Keep headings uniform. Use smaller sizes on subheads to indicate relative importance.

- Use only a few lines of type on any slide.

- Use color on charts and graphs to add interest.

- Double-check everything to make sure it is in proper order.

- Make the room as dark as possible.

- Use a screen, not a wall. Make sure the screen is large enough for everyone to see.

- Everything on a slide must be visible to the people in the last row. Take a look at your visuals from the back of the room.

- Tape down the projector cord so no one will trip on it.

- Make sure the projector and screen are properly aligned.

- Leave each slide on the screen long enough for everyone to read and understand it and for you to make your point, then move on to the next one. The audience's interest will flag if a slide is left on too long.

Videotapes

- Don't be afraid to use emotional appeal. Videotapes are uniquely suited to offering "slice of life" material. For example, if you're giving a speech on the need to donate blood, try a short videotape showing the people who benefit from blood donations. Get close-ups of faces, of children holding their parents' hands, of doctors comforting patients. Don't use "perfect" people. Use "real" people who look like your audience.

- Make sure the tapes are compatible with the available playback units.

- Have enough monitors available. The audience should not have to strain to see your videotape.

- Check and adjust each monitor in advance.

Audiotapes

- Audiotapes are excellent for presenting new radio jingles, public service announcements, or short messages from focus groups—to name just a few uses.

- Jack your playback unit directly into the room's sound system.

Emergency A-V Kit

Even with careful preparation, lots of things can go wrong when you use audiovisual materials. Prepare an emergency kit and carry it to all presentations. Include:

- extension cords
- spare light bulbs
- three-pronged adapters
- a multiple-outlet box
- masking tape
- scissors, screwdriver, pliers
- a small flashlight

HOW TO PREPARE YOURSELF

When you give a speech, you want to look your best, sound your best, and feel your best. Don't leave these things to chance.

How to Look Your Best

Don't wear brand-new clothes to give a speech. New clothes haven't had a chance to "fit" your body. They often feel stiff and uncomfortable, and what could be worse than having a button pop off or a seam rip open when you gesture in the middle of your speech? Wear "old favorites" instead—clothes that fit well and move the way *you* move.

Dress conservatively for most business functions. If in doubt about the suitability of a piece of clothing, don't wear it. Your appearance should not interfere with your message. Or, as Cary Grant's father put it, "Let them see *you* and not the suit."

For men: A dark suit—clean and well-pressed, of course. (Navy blue or "banker's" blue is generally a color that conveys authority and elicits trust.) A long-sleeved shirt. (White or blue look best under bright lights.) A conservative tie with a touch of red for power (an old politician's trick). Long, dark socks. (The audience shouldn't see a patch of hairy leg when you sit down and cross your legs.) Well-shined shoes. No pens sticking out of your shirt pocket, please. And no coins or keys bulging in your pants pockets.

For women: A suit or a dress (static-free and non-cling, of course). For soft touches, a bit of lace or a ruffle on your blouse. No low necklines. Be especially careful with your hemline if you will be seated on stage before you speak. Moderate heels—no spiked heels that will clomp as you cross a wooden floor. And no rattling jewelry. Arrange to leave your purse with someone in the audience. Do not carry it to the podium.

How to Sound Your Best

Treat your voice well. No cheering for the local football team the day before.

Try using a humidifier the night before. If you're staying in a hotel room, fill the bathtub with water before going to sleep. Moisture in the air will help prevent a dry-throat feeling.

Hot tea with honey and lemon is great for the voice. Use herbal tea for an extra calming effect. Chamomile tea can be particularly relaxing.

How to Feel Your Best

On the day before a big speech:

- Don't decide to get a totally new hair style. What would happen if you hated it?

- Don't decide to start that intensive exercise program you've been talking about for months. A brisk walk around the park? Fine. A five-mile run? Insane. Who wants aches and pains to deal with on top of everything else?

- Don't decide to "paint the town red." Wait until *after* the speech to have a few drinks. You'll feel better about yourself.

ELEVEN

Delivery

❧

All the great speakers were bad speakers at first.
—Ralph Waldo Emerson

Practice makes perfect, the saying goes. Well, practice may not make you a perfect speaker, but it will certainly make you a better speaker. With the right coaching, you may even become a great speaker.

This chapter will coach you on:

- executive presence
- voice control
- eye contact
- body language

It will also show you how to deal with two special concerns: nervousness and hecklers.

PRACTICING YOUR DELIVERY

Practice your *delivery,* not just your speech.

It's not enough to know the *content* of your speech. You

must also be comfortable with the gestures and pauses and emphases that will help get your message across to the audience.

To do this, practice the speech in four stages. First, familiarize yourself with the script itself. Then familiarize yourself with the delivery techniques you'll need.

1. *Begin by reading the speech aloud to yourself.* Tape record it. How long does it take? Where do you need to pause to avoid running out of breath in mid-sentence? Should you rewrite any sentences so they're easier to deliver? Do you need to vary your pace?

   How does your voice sound? Does it fade at the end of sentences?

   If you generally have trouble projecting your voice, try putting the tape recorder across the room while you practice. This trick should *force* you to speak louder.

2. *Deliver the speech standing in front of a mirror.* By now, you should be familiar enough with the material to look up from the manuscript fairly often. Concentrate on emphasizing the right parts. See how your face becomes more animated at certain points in the speech.

   Caution: Be sure to rehearse the entire speech each time you practice. Otherwise, you'll have a well-prepared beginning but a weak ending.

   Deny yourself the luxury of "backtracking." If you make a mistake during rehearsal—trip on a line or leave something out—don't go back and start again. Be realistic. How would you recover from a mistake in front of an audience? That's how you should recover from it during your rehearsal.

3. *Deliver the speech to a friend.* Try to simulate a realistic environment. Stand up. Use a lectern. Arrange some chairs.

If you need to put on glasses to see the script, now's the time to practice doing that unobtrusively. Practice moving the pages quietly to the side. Don't "flip" them over. Look at your listener.

By this point, you should have memorized the first fifteen seconds of your speech and the last fifteen seconds, moments when eye contact is most critical. Do *not* try to memorize the rest of the speech, or your delivery will sound stilted. Focus on the ideas, not the words. Just look up a lot to make sure you're getting those ideas across. It's this eye contact with an audience that animates a speaker.

Allow yourself to smile when it feels natural. Gesture with your hand to make a point. Let your face talk, too.

4. *Practice again before a small group.* Try to make good eye contact with each person. Play with your voice a little bit to keep your listeners' attention. Notice where it helps to speak faster, slower, louder, softer. If possible, practice in the room in which you will speak.

If you haven't been able to rehearse on-site, arrive early enough to get comfortable with the layout before you speak.

PRESENCE

A speech doesn't start when you begin to speak. It starts the moment you enter the room.

An audience will start to form an opinion of you as soon as they see you. First impressions count. Make yours good.

Carry yourself with presence from the moment you arrive. Be well groomed. Don't carry loose papers. Walk in a brisk, businesslike manner. Be polite to receptionists and secretaries. They may tell their bosses about you later. It's fruitless to talk to an audience about corporate ethics if they've heard you be rude to the receptionist.

Listen carefully to other speakers and respond appropriately. Pay particular attention to the person who introduces you.

All eyes will be on you as you walk to the podium, so don't be buttoning your jacket or sorting your papers. Take care of those details *before* you leave your chair.

Don't bother to hide the fact that you'll use a written text. Just carry the speech at your side—not in front of your chest, where it looks like a protective shield. If you plan to shake hands with the person who introduced you, carry the speech in your other hand so you don't have to make a last-minute switch.

Never place your speech on the lectern in advance. Someone speaking ahead of you might carry it away accidentally, and then you'd be stuck.

When you get to the lectern, take care of "The Big Six"— preparations you can't afford to skip.

1. Open your folder and remove the paper clip from your speech.

2. Make sure the lectern is at a comfortable level. You should, of course, have adjusted it in advance, but if another speaker has changed the height, now's the time to correct it.

3. Check the position of the microphone. Again, you should have tested the microphone in advance. Check the switch. If you question the level, just say, "Testing—1, 2, 3." *Do not blow into the microphone or tap it.*

4. Stand straight and place your weight evenly over both feet. This will help you feel "grounded" and in control of the situation.

5. *Look* at the audience before you start to speak. This pause will quiet them and give you a chance to . . .

6. . . . Breathe!

Now, you're ready to speak.

VOICE

Demosthenes, the Athenian orator, supposedly practiced speaking with a mouth full of pebbles. You don't have to go to such extremes.

When you rehearse your speech, check these basics:

- *Rate.*   Time yourself with a stopwatch. How many words do you speak in a minute? Most people speak in public at about 150 words per minute.
- *Variety.*   Can you vary your pace? Slower to set a particular mood? Faster to create excitement?
- *Emphasis.*   Do you emphasize the right words and phrases?
- *Volume.*   Can people hear you? If not, open your mouth more.
- *Rhythm.*   Do all your sentences sound alike? Do you habitually drop your voice at the end of a sentence?
- *Fillers.*   Do you ruin the flow of your thoughts with "uh" and "er" and "ah"?
- *Clarity.*   Do you slur your contractions *(wu'nt* for *wouldn't)*? Do you reverse sounds (*per*scription for *pre*-scription)? Do you omit sounds (lis*t*s)?; Do you add sounds (acros*t*)?

If you have serious speech problems, get professional help. Many colleges and universities have excellent speech clinics. Take advantage of them.

EYE CONTACT

Good eye contact will do more to help your delivery than anything else.

When you *look* at people, they believe you care about them. They believe you are sincere. They believe you are honest. How can you go wrong if an audience feels this way about you?

Really *look* at the people in your audience—and look at them as *individuals*. Don't look over their heads or stare at some vague spot in the back of the room. Don't "sweep" the room with your eyes. Instead, look directly at one person until you finish a thought, then move on to another. You must maintain good eye contact with the audience if you are going to convey sincerity.

Avoid looking repeatedly at the same person. It's best to look at as many individuals as possible in the time allowed.

Eye contact will also give you instantaneous feedback. Does the audience look interested or are they nodding out? If you sense boredom, intensify your eye contact, vary your voice, use body language.

Try not to look up at the audience during grammatical pauses (for example, between sentences) because physical movement seems awkward when there's nothing verbal going on.

BODY LANGUAGE

Most books on public speaking talk about the importance of gestures. I prefer to talk about the importance of *body language*. It is, of course, important to gesture with your hands if you want to make a point. But it's just as important to speak *with your whole body*.

A raised eyebrow, a smile, a shrug of the shoulders—they all make a statement. If you use them wisely, they can contribute a lot to your speech.

It's not necessary (or even advisable) to choreograph your body movements in advance. You'll find that they spring naturally from your message, from your belief in what you're saying. If you put energy and thought and life into your message, your body movements will take good care of themselves. If you *don't,* no amount of hand-waving will help your cause.

As you rehearse and deliver your speech:

- You'll find yourself leaning forward slightly to make a stronger point.
- You'll find yourself smiling when you quote something amusing.
- You'll find yourself gesturing with your whole arm, not just with a finger or a flick of the wrist.
- You'll find yourself nodding slightly when you sense a good response from the audience.
- You'll find yourself shaking your head when you cite something that's offensive or inaccurate.

You'll find yourself, in short, developing charisma. The more energy you *give* to an audience, the more charisma you will develop. It's an exchange—you give and you get.

A word of caution about gestures. No feeble ones, please. If you raise just a finger to make a point, the audience may not even see the gesture. Raise your whole hand. Raise your whole arm. Make your movements *say* something.

If you have trouble expressing yourself physically, swing your arms in figure-eights before you speak. (In privacy, of course.) This big movement will loosen you up.

WHEN YOU FINISH SPEAKING

You've just spoken the last word of your speech. *Be careful.* Your speech isn't really over. Don't walk away from the podium yet. Hold your position. Look directly at the audience for a few more seconds. Remain in control of the silence just as you remained in control of the speech.

If you wrote a good speech, your final words were strong and memorable. In fact, your ending was probably the best part of the whole speech. Allow it to sink in.

Then, close your folder and walk away from the podium. Walk briskly and confidently—the same way you approached the podium.

When you take your seat, do *not* start talking to the person next to you. Someone else is probably at the podium now, and the audience would think it rude for you to be talking.

Above all, don't say things like, "Whew, am I glad *that's* over," or "Could you see how much my hands were trembling?" I have even seen speakers sit down and roll their eyes and shake their heads—a sure way to detract from an otherwise good speech.

Just sit quietly. Look attentive and confident.

There may well be applause. Smile and look pleased to be there. It would seem unnatural to act any other way.

Some speakers—those with a lot at stake—even plan their applause. They make sure that staff members attend the speech —not sitting together, but spread throughout the audience. When these people start to applaud, they produce a ripple effect. Voilà! A standing ovation!

NERVOUSNESS

"I'm afraid I'll be nervous."

That's a common feeling, and in some ways it's healthy. It shows you care about getting your message across to the audience. You really *do* want to look and sound good.

But it's important to understand what nervousness is. Nervousness is simply *energy.* If you channel that energy, you can turn it into a positive force. You can make it work for you. You can use the extra energy to your advantage.

But if you allow that energy to go unchecked—if you allow *it* to control *you*—then you're going to have problems. A dry mouth, perhaps, or a cracking voice. Lots of rocking back and forth on your feet, or lots of "uh's" and "um's." Maybe even forgetfulness.

How can you channel your nervous energy?

By taking the advice that appears in this chapter. Learn to direct your extra energy into eye contact, body language, vocal enthusiasm. These physical activities provide an outlet for your nervousness. They offer a way to use up some of that extra energy.

What's more, good eye contact, strong body language, and vocal enthusiasm will build your *confidence.* It's hard to feel insecure when you look directly at your listeners and see the responsiveness in their faces.

Pre-Speech Tricks to Prevent Nervousness

There are tricks to every trade, and public speaking is no exception. Do what the pros do to keep their nervousness in check.

- *Try physical exercises.*

   Just before you speak, go off by yourself (to the restroom or to a quiet corner) and concentrate on the part of your body that feels most tense. Your face? Your hands? Your stomach? Deliberately tighten that part even more until it starts to quiver, then let go. You will feel an enormous sense of relief. Repeat this a few times.

   Drop your head. Let your cheek muscles go loose and let your mouth go slack.

Make funny faces. Puff up your cheeks, then let the air escape. Or open your mouth and your eyes wide, then close them tightly. Alternate a few times.

Yawn a few times to loosen your jaw and your mucous membranes.

Pretend you're an opera singer. Try "mi, mi, mi" a few times. Wave your arms as you do it.

- *Try mental exercises.*

Picture something that's given you pleasant memories. Sailing on a blue-green ocean. Swimming in a mountain lake. Walking on a beach, feeling the sand between your toes. (Water often has a calming effect on people.)

- *Try a rational approach.*

Say to yourself, "I'm prepared. I know what I'm talking about." Or, "I've spent a year working on this project. Nobody knows as much about this project as I do." Or, "I'm glad I can talk to these people. It will help my career."

I know someone who repeats to herself, "This is better than death, this is better than death." That may sound extreme, but it works for her. And, she's right. Giving a speech *is* better than death.

If you're scared to give a speech, try to think of something that's *really* frightening. The speech should seem appealing by comparison.

- *Try a test run.*

Visualize exactly what will happen after you're introduced. You'll get out of your chair, you'll hold the folder in your left hand, you'll walk confidently across the stage, you'll hold your head high, you'll look directly at the person who introduced you, you'll shake his or her hand, you'll . . .

*If you see yourself as confident and successful in your
mental test run, you'll be confident and successful in your
delivery.*

Above all, never *say* that you're nervous. If you do, you'll
make yourself more nervous. And you'll make the audience
nervous, too.

During-the-Speech Tricks to Overcome Nervousness

Okay. You've prepared your speech carefully. You've done the
pre-speech exercises. Now you're at the podium and—can that
be?—your mouth goes a little dry.

Don't panic. Just intensify your eye contact. Looking at the
audience will take away your self-preoccupation and reduce the
dryness.

Persistent dryness? Help yourself to the glass of water that
you've wisely placed at the lectern. Don't be embarrassed. Say
to yourself, "It's my speech, and I can damned well drink water
if I want to."

What else can go wrong because of misplaced nervous energy? I once found that my teeth got so dry, my lips actually
stuck to them. An actor friend later told me to rub a light
coating of Vaseline over my teeth. It's a good tip.

Other mini-traumas?

• *Sweat rolling off your forehead.* Wipe it away with the
  big cotton handkerchief that you also placed at the lectern.
  Don't hesitate to really *wipe*. Little dabs are ineffectual,
  and you'll have to dab repeatedly. Do it right the first time,
  and get it over with. Also, avoid using tissues. They can
  shred and get stuck on your face—not a terribly impressive sight.

- *A quivery voice.*   Again, intensify your eye contact. Focus on *them*. Then lower your pitch and control your breath as you begin to speak. Concentrate on speaking distinctly and slowly.

- *Shaking hands.*   Take heart. The audience probably can't see your trembling hands, but if they're distracting you, then use some body movement to diffuse that nervous energy. Change your foot position. Lean forward to make a point. Move your arms. (If your body is in a frozen position, your shaking will only grow worse.)

- *A pounding heart.*   No, the audience *cannot* see the rising and falling of your chest.

- *Throat clearing.*   If you have to cough, cough—away from the microphone. Drink some water, or pop a cough drop into your mouth. Again, the well-prepared speaker has an unwrapped cough drop handy at all times—and ready to use.

- *Runny nose, watery eyes.*   Bright lights can trigger these responses. Simply pause, say "Excuse me," blow your nose or wipe your eyes, and get on with it. Don't make a big deal over it by apologizing. A simple "Excuse me" is just fine.

- *Nausea.*   You come down with a viral infection two days before your speech and you're afraid of throwing up in the middle of it. Well, that's why they make anti-nausea drugs. Ask your doctor about a prescription.

  For actors, the show must always go on . . . even with serious viral infections. More than one actor has placed a trash can backstage so he could throw up between acts. But *you* are not an actor, and you really don't have to put yourself through this test of will power. If you are terribly ill—as opposed to being just mildly nervous—cancel your engagement. Since you've prepared a complete manuscript, perhaps a colleague could substitute for you. If substitution is not possible, offer to speak at a later date.

• *Burping.*   Some people feel they have to burp when they get nervous. If you are one of these people, do plenty of physical relaxation exercises before you speak. Don't drink any carbonated beverages that day, and eat only a light lunch.

• *Fumbled words.*   Professional speakers, radio announcers, and television anchorpeople fumble words fairly often. Why should you expect to be perfect?

If it's a minor fumble, just ignore it and keep going.

If it's a big one, fix it. Simply repeat the correct word —with a smile, to show you're human.

Continue with your speech, but slow down a little bit. Once you've had a slip of the tongue, chances are high you'll have another. A fumble is a sort of symptom that you're focusing more on yourself than on your message. Relax and slow down.

• *Forgetfulness.*   Some people look at an audience and forget what they want to say. Aren't you glad you made the effort to prepare a good written manuscript? It's all right there, so you have one less thing to worry about.

HECKLERS

Hecklers tend to exist only in the bad dreams of speakers. They almost never pose real-life problems.

But if you are in the middle of your speech and you see someone waving an arm at you, then you need real-life help. And fast.

First of all, stay calm. Hecklers are like people who make obscene telephone calls. They just love to upset you. If you stay calm, you destroy their pleasure. If you stay calm, you also stay in control.

Ignore the hand that's waving in the air and keep right on speaking. It takes a lot of energy to wave a hand in the air, and the person will probably grow tired and give up. (Try waving your hand in the air for a few minutes, and you'll see what I mean.)

If you hear a voice? Stop speaking, remain calm, and ask the person to hold the question until after your speech. Be polite but firm. The audience will respect your approach and the person will most likely respect your request. Proceed with your speech.

If the person gets louder, you should *not* continue. Look instead at the person who organized this speaking engagement. If you're lucky, that person will come to your aid and quiet the heckler or escort him out of the room.

If not, speak to the heckler again. Say, "As I said before, I'll be glad to answer all questions *after* my speech." By now, your patience and professionalism should have earned the respect—and sympathy—of the rest of the audience.

If the heckling worsens, confront the person. Say, "Everyone here knows I'm *(name)* and I'm from the *(name)* company. Could you tell us who *you* are?" Hecklers, like obscene phone callers, almost certainly prefer to remain anonymous.

If the tirade continues, you will have to count on the audience for their support. Stop speaking, and step back from the podium. Let *them* put pressure on the heckler to shut up or leave.

After all, *you* are the invited speaker, not the heckler. You shouldn't have to justify your presence. You have a right to be treated fairly and to get your message across. If the audience isn't willing to support your basic rights, then don't waste your time trying to speak to them.

Leave—with dignity.

And remember: Your chances of meeting a real-life heckler are slim. Don't lose any sleep over it.

T W E L V E

Media Coverage

>

Veni, video, vici.
I came, I appeared on television, I conquered.

Your speech probably won't merit coverage on network television news, but there are lots of other ways to get good publicity for your speech.

Start small and work your way up the publicity scale. Begin with the basics and do as much as your budget and your time will allow—and, yes, as much as your *material* will allow.

Face it. Not all speeches are newsworthy. If you expect the media to pay attention to a routine speech, you will be disappointed.

Here are nine ways to get good publicity for your speech:

1. *Give it a catchy title.* Come up with titles that *beg* to be quoted.

    Need ideas? Try variations on the titles of popular movies, books and songs. Be specific. Be graphic. Be irreverent if you want. Just don't be boring.

    Consider these examples:

    • "Wouldn't It Be Great, Just Once, If the World Scheduled a Crisis—And We Didn't Come?" (from Robert J. Buckley, chairman of Allegheny International, Inc.)

- "A Most Ingenious Paradox" (from David M. Roderick, chairman of United States Steel Corporation; based on a line from a Gilbert and Sullivan song)

- "Making Love in Public" (from John R. Bonée of Illinois Bell, on public relations and bank marketing)

- "High Tech with Dirty Fingernails: American Industry's Last Chance" (from James A. Baker, executive vice president of General Electric)

Avoid titles that sound like doctoral dissertations (e.g., "The Inherent Challenges of Economic Redistribution in the 1980s"). Nobody wants to quote anything that sounds like a textbook.

2. *Distribute copies to the audience.*   Always do this *after* your presentation, not before. Otherwise, they'll be reading and rustling papers while you're trying to speak.

One good way: have assistants at the doors as the audience leaves.

3. *Give a copy to your employee information staff.*   Your public relations department may be able to plan a related story for the employee newspaper.

4. *Send an advance copy of the speech to the trade publication that serves your business.*   Make the editor's work easier:

- Be sure the speech is easy to read—with short paragraphs and wide margins. (See chapter 10 for details.) Add subheads to catch the editor's attention.

- Use colored ink to underline a couple of quotable phrases in the speech—phrases the editor can pull out and use in a caption or headline or call-out.

- Attach a one-page summary. This summary may be the only thing the editor bothers to read, so make it good.

Highlight the speech's main points. Include an impressive statistic or a memorable quote or an interesting example—anything to grab the editor's attention.

5. *Send an advance copy to nearby colleges and universities.*

• The placement office may want to file your speech and share it with students who apply to your company.

• The appropriate department may want to present your ideas in class.

• The campus newspaper may want to cover your speech, especially if its content affects the lives of students.

6. *Prepare news releases for newspapers and local radio/TV stations.* Make your releases short and snappy. Don't think "corporate." Think "newsworthy/interesting/important." Put yourself in the shoes of an editor or a news director and ask, "What kind of press release would I like to receive?" The universal answer: "The kind of press release that makes my work easier."

For newspapers: Give them a good lead, something they can use "as is." Editors aren't looking for more work. They're looking for good stories to make their work easier. Give them a good lead, and they may give you good coverage.

For radio and TV: Give them three or four short sentences written for the ear and ready to deliver on the air. Remember: News directors receive dozens—often hundreds—of press releases each day. It's human nature for them to use the ones that are "ready to go"—that don't require research and rewriting.

Mail the press releases a few days in advance. Be sure to provide round-the-clock telephone numbers where the editor or news director can contact you.

Note: Many of the smaller radio stations will play excerpts of major speeches. Send them a tape.

7. *Appear on a radio or TV interview program.* The United States has about 800 commercial TV stations and about 8,000 AM and FM radio stations—plus about 5,000 cable stations. Virtually all of them have interview programs where you can appear as a follow-up to your speech. (*Note:* Don't underestimate the smaller, non-prime-time shows. They may give you valuable access to certain audiences.)

How can you get booked for an interview program? Call the station about two weeks in advance and let the program director know why the story is newsworthy. Be brief. Program directors have busy schedules and won't listen to a long-winded pitch.

If you sense interest, offer written backup material. Include any recent publications. A book or a magazine feature will increase your credibility. For TV shows, offer to provide visuals—slides, film footage, small-scale models, even documents to lift and show as you make your point.

Television is a highly visual medium. If you offer to show things to the viewers, you will stand a better chance of getting on the show.

8. *Reprint the speech and take a direct-mail approach.* It is quite inexpensive to issue speech reprints on standard-size business paper with holes punched for easy insertion into loose-leaf binders.

If your budget allows, you might want to publish a booklet with a bold cover.

Of course, you don't have to reprint the entire speech. Avon once *condensed* a talk on corporate support for volunteerism and published just these highlights in a glossy brochure entitled "Caring . . . Is Everyone's Business." The brochure used only one 8½ × 11–inch piece of glossy paper, folded into thirds—handy for fitting into a standard #10 business envelope.

Be sure to consider postage costs when you design your reprints.

9. *Submit a copy to* Vital Speeches. *Vital Speeches* is a magazine that reprints important speeches on a variety of topics. Mail your speech to:

- VITAL SPEECHES
  City News Publishing Company
  Box 606
  Southold, NY 11971

You may also want to submit copies to:

- SPEECHWRITER'S NEWSLETTER
  407 South Dearborn
  Chicago, IL 60605

- THE EXECUTIVE SPEAKER
  P.O. Box 2094
  Dayton, OH 45429

Make the most of your speech. After all, you worked hard to prepare it. Now, make it work hard for *you*.

Index